*Okay, Let's Try It Again*

ALSO BY WILLEM LANGE

*Not Love at First Sight* (audio tape)  1998

*Tales from the Edge of the Woods*  1998

*John and Tom*  2001

*Where Does the Wild Goose Go?*  2002

*Intermittent Bliss*  2003

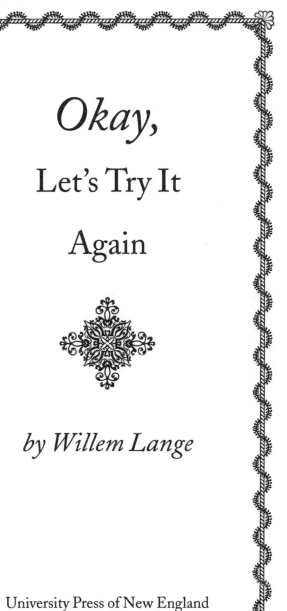

# *Okay,*

## Let's Try It

## Again

*by Willem Lange*

University Press of New England

HANOVER AND LONDON

University Press of New England, 37 Lafayette St., Lebanon, NH 03766

© 1999 by Willem Lange

Printed in the United States of America

5   4   3   2

CIP data appear at the end of the book

The pieces in this book first appeared in the *Valley News*, Lebanon, New Hampshire. Many of them, edited for radio, also have been aired by the author on Vermont Public Radio as part of his regular commentary series.

IN LOVING MEMORY OF

BILL AND CHARLIE BROE

# Contents

CONTENTS

# Introduction

For over fifty years I have drawn refreshment for my spirit from the wild places of my world. I have stumbled through rhododendron hells of the Great Smoky Mountains and the knee-deep tundra of the Great Barren Lands. My friends and I have paddled icy Arctic rivers in Canada, hunted deer in the high peaks of the Adirondacks, and carried tiny boats through the woods to almost-forgotten trout ponds. All of this—even the cold, the rain and snow, the smoky fires, the bugs—have been so precious a part of my life that at times they seem to comprise the sum of it.

But it hasn't always been that way. As a child, I lived in Albany, New York, only a few blocks from the State Capitol. The only green or growing things in view from our building were the ornamental trees planted in their little pits of dirt in the sidewalk. There were animals: the horses that pulled the wagons of the men delivering bread, eggs, milk, and coal, and of the men, straight from Dickens novels, picking up rags and scrap metal. But the only wild animals were big gray rats and the fierce feral cats that hunted them in the canyons between buildings. Flocks of sparrows fed upon the manure left in the streets by the horses; pigeons were everywhere; and one year there was a nest of kestrels on our fourth-floor windowsill.

All that changed when I was eight years old and we moved to central New York, to an outside edge of a geometrically patterned city and the nether edge of what seemed to me infinite green possibilities. It was the beginning of a lifelong love affair with wild places. They have meant everything to me, and I like to think I have been a thoughtful and considerate lover.

But there was one surprise for me, when I began to go outdoors. Some friends of mine and I had discovered a tiny stream, well out of the city, full of bright native brook trout—a bubbling little fountain running through a deep hemlock forest. I yearned to have it all for myself. So on a Friday afternoon after school, I took a city bus downtown to the interurban depot and climbed onto a bus headed east. An hour or so later I got off at an empty crossroads several miles from my stream. Loaded with an army pup tent, a can or two of beans, matches, a blanket, and my fishing pole, I hiked to the stream and set up camp as darkness fell around me.

All night long I lay awake. Next to my tent, curious cows gathered to sniff and moo and chew their cuds. A whippoorwill sang beautifully, interminably. The brook bubbled by my tent, and it seemed to me that I could hear voices, but never quite what they were saying. In the morning, instead of fishing and staying the second night, I packed my gear and hiked back to the bus line. It took me years to understand what had happened: I was lonesome.

Wild places, by simplifying our environment and

removing our usual distractions, can teach us quickly—if we are alive to the lessons—what it might otherwise take us a lifetime to learn. And I have noticed, looking back now even beyond that night, how much my joy in people has run as an unbroken bright thread through the whole fabric of my life.

The stories in this collection are about some of those people who in the last fifty years and more have brightened or darkened—but always enlarged—my life. They are my constant companions on the luminous little brooks of memory.

## Okay, Let's Try It Again

# Okay, Let's Try It Again

DURING THE FIRST YEAR OF THE WAR, little banners began to appear in the front windows of American homes. Rimmed in red, with a white field in the middle, they bore one blue star for each member of the family in the armed forces. Many had more than one star. As the war went on and on, some of those stars changed to gold, to show that the serviceperson had died. Again, some had more than one gold star. There were dozens of them scattered through the neighborhoods of our city. We kids, whose contributions to the war effort consisted of collecting newspapers, scrap metal, milkweed pods (for life vests), and lard, and buying defense stamps in school, never passed one of those homes without lowering our voices, peeking sideways at the stars in embarrassment at someone else's sacrifice, and trying to imagine the heartbreak inside.

Finally the nightmare ended. None of us knew quite what had happened at those Japanese cities with names we had never heard before, but it didn't matter at the time. It was over! No more rationing; no more air raid drills; and the city buses stopped again on every corner. The country heaved a vast, collective sigh, and our armed forces came home with a grinning swagger.

Within a year—about the time I was finally old enough to join the Boy Scouts—the Scout troops of America were led by men who were veterans of the war. They were still pretty military and very tough cookies. Not ours!

His nickname was Doc, probably because he looked a lot like Doc in *Snow White and the Seven Dwarfs*. Unathletic, round-shouldered, and bespectacled, he didn't look as though he could survive a tennis match, let alone a war. And he never seemed to get anything right.

He almost always gave the command, "Harch!" on the wrong foot, and the whole troop got tangled up. We marched nervously back and forth across the Lutheran church basement where we held our meetings, our ears straining, awaiting the moment of the miscued command. It was like waiting for the guillotine blade to drop. One visiting Scout executive described us as resembling "a spastic centipede."

Doc's favorite expression, necessarily, was, "Okay, let's try it again."

We went camping at least one weekend every month. Whenever we saw Doc collecting his double handful of dry ragweed to start the campfire, we knew he'd need help before he was done. He normally went through a book of matches without producing a fire. One of us would go for more tinder, others would start splitting kindling, and the rest would saw up chunks of dead apple branches.

His cooking was unbelievable, inedible, even unidentifiable. The bacon was cinders, the scrambled eggs sawdust, the toast pure carbon. But that was nothing compared to his specialty, which he called

Spanish rice. There was always plenty left over, in a pot too burned to wash till morning. And when the little forest folk came out at night to forage around the campsite, they walked in circles around that pot. But none of them, not even the porcupines, would touch it.

Purely in self-defense, several of us, with the help and advice of our mothers at home, became fairly competent camp cooks.

"Today," he once announced in his teacherly tones as we washed up the breakfast dishes, "today we are going to learn to use the map and compass to find our way across trackless territory." If we had listened more carefully, we might have heard the key words, "*we* are going to learn." Within two hours' time, *we* were so lost that some of the new kids began to cry.

We spread out our map on a patch of gravel. "Where are we, Doc?" we asked.

"Hmm, I don't know. We've been traveling at 127 degrees, I think, so we ought to be about—here. But it sure doesn't look like that here, does it? What do you think?"

We pored over the map, walked several more hours, and somehow found our way back to camp before dark. "You must be tired," said Doc. "I'll start supper."

"No, no, no!" we cried. "We'll take care of it!"

We built log bridges, watchtowers, and Adirondack leantos; we fitted our permanent campsite with an altar fireplace, which eliminated bending over to cook. We carved willow pothooks, built a first-class privy, planted thousands of trees and multiflora roses for small game cover. We carried Indian tanks of trout to stock remote forest ponds (which we found with map and compass) and helped set out young pheasants. We collected newspapers to get money for new tents. We practiced for marching competition without Doc, who seemed relieved to be out of it. As we thrashed our own way through everything, our slogan became, "Okay, let's try it again!"

Through it all, from Tenderfoot to First Class to Eagle, we carried the poor guy. He was competent to drive us to the edge of the woods, but after that we had to watch out for him. He was hopeless. How he'd ever survived we couldn't imagine.

Only a few of us ever noticed, behind those gold-rimmed bifocals, the quiet twinkle in his eyes. And whenever anyone of us was feeling down—homesick, maybe, or dying from that other great Boy Scout ailment, diarrhea—old Doc would somehow be sitting there next to him at the campfire. If it was dark and raining, or swarming with mosquitoes, whoever had the pots-and-pans scrubbing detail would find Doc's bulky figure squatting beside him at the brook with a Chore Boy in his hand. "Here! Give me some of those pots," he'd say.

Over the past fifty years, as often I've thought of him, I've remembered best his awkward, round-shouldered way of saluting as we weekly pledged, "On my honor I will do my best to do my duty to God and my country . . . to keep myself physically strong, mentally awake, and morally straight.. And each time I try, and fail, I murmur to his imaginary presence, "I'm sorry, Doc."

And each time, his ghost smiles and replies, "Okay, let's try it again."

# Mrs. Sandwick

It was 1946. The United States was briefly between wars and, according to my parents, between Presidents, as well. I was in the sixth grade.

Mrs. Sandwick's desk was in the left front corner of the room, beside the windows and guarding the door to the supply room. Her promenade, when she used it, was the twenty-foot-long strip of oiled wood floor up front, between the blackboard and the front seats. She rarely came down the rows, among us; instead, she controlled from up front virtually everything that happened in that room, as surely as a coachman with eight horses in hand.

I sat toward the back in the center. My view of Mrs. Sandwick's pink-rouged face, stern glasses, and gold-dyed hair was always through the heads and shoulders of my classmates. (There was a rumor among us that she had once been in the Ziegfeld Follies—whatever that was.) I sat right behind Catherine Coburn, whose ginger-brown braids I longed to dip into my inkwell. But I would have died before doing such a thing; for I would surely have died afterward.

She ruled our classroom with the moral conviction of Jonathan Edwards and the ferocity of the Emperor Caligula. Each morning at precisely 8:45 she was delivered to the east side of Bellevue Heights School by a 1939 black Chevrolet sedan. Carrying a brocade shopping bag in one hand and her school shoes in the other, she marched firmly up the walk and through the high portal. If one of us was near the door when she reached it, there was no question but that he would open it with a polite, embarrassed flourish. "Thank you," she said, with a slight nod of her head. After the door had closed behind her, the Chevy pulled away.

If we looked up then toward the windows of our second-floor classroom—and who could resist?—we could watch most of her morning routine. First she straightened out what she called "the mess left by the janitor" the night before, pulling all the window shades up or down to precisely uniform heights. Then we saw fluttering fabric as she shook the dust covers of her desk, the globe, and her bookcase. Her head disappeared from our view as she sat down and bent to don her school shoes; reappeared as she put her street shoes into the supply closet; and then disappeared again as she went to her station by the hall door to greet us and, by her manner, remind us of the decorum required in her classroom.

It seemed a very long year! Sixth grade had been chosen by the school system as the year during which kids would learn proper penmanship, would learn all their single-number arithmetical tables, would learn to spell correctly any words they might conceivably use during the next decade, and would learn to use the library. I do not use "would be taught," but "would learn." The first was taken for granted, and Mrs. Sandwick performed it with a vengeance. She also saw to it that we in turn performed our part of the transaction with appropriate diligence.

Following the Pledge to the Flag and a brief reading from the Bible each morning, there came penmanship. Mrs. Sandwick had made each of us a heavily lined template to place under our writing paper—in those days before copying machines, had made them one by one with pen and ruler! The template's parallel lines were slanted at the proper Palmer Method angle. We dipped straight pens into inkwells all together and began the first of countless *O*'s and "staffs" to her metronomic beat. It was required that our whole arms move during this exercise, not just our wrists and fingers. She left her promenade in the front of the room, still clapping her hands to the beat, and circulated up and down the aisles, clasping "lazy elbows" in her steely grip and pumping them lustily back and forth. I don't remember who, if anybody, didn't hate it.

Nor do I recall anymore the exact progression of subjects after penmanship. But at least once in every day we had arithmetic flash cards, composition, grammar, spelling, vocabulary, and library period. A lot of our learning was competitive: for example, she pitted the seven rows in the classroom against each other in flash card speed drills. I don't want to accuse her of stacking the deck or anything, but somehow I always seemed to get the one I found most difficult, seven times eight. Then we'd choose sides for spelling bees or vocabulary quizzes.

In the back of her classroom Mrs. Sandwick kept a glass-fronted library of several hundred volumes. She appointed librarians, and each day for twenty minutes we were allowed—I should say expected—to take out or exchange books. She and her appointees were punctilious about the proper care of the volumes, and assessed damages for any untoward wear. "All your friends may fail you someday," she would say (and I wonder sometimes now, remembering, whether that awful thing had happened to her), "but as long as you have a book, you have a friend who will never fail you. So learn to treat them well." She showed us how to open a new book for the first time, and I have done it just that way, almost reverently, for over fifty years.

What a relief it was when at last, at the end of our long nine months together, we received from Mrs. Sandwick the report card that elevated us to junior high school and freed us from her tyranny forever! Or so we thought.

Now, there are some who may read this with horror at such teaching, or with sympathy for the wretched urchins under the whip of such a Dickensian despot. Most of us born before World War II can remember teachers like her. I hope others remember theirs with the same fondness and nostalgia with which I remember Mrs. Sandwick.

Because there was another side to this grim coin. True, we had to endure her inflexible regimen just at a time when our animal sap was rising irresistibly and brighter visions beckoned. But like metal braces on wandering teeth, Mrs. Sandwick's iron hand helped dictate a course for us that has lasted far beyond high school and college. Just a few paragraphs back, I felt that hand, light as a feather now, touch my shoulder as I typed the word *conceivably (i* before *e* except after *c,* or when sounded . . . ).

Consider that she had thirty-six twelve-year-old savages to subdue and educate each day (well, maybe thirty-four. There's no way that Catherine Coburn or Albert Kallfelz could ever have been savages. But the rest of us were full of it). We were a heterogeneous mob ethnically, theologically, economically, and intellectually; and she was committed to achieving the sixth-grade objectives with every one of us. Thus the competitions and the teams: we coached each other during study time. Thus the library in the back of the room. I found out years later that because the school couldn't afford a library, Mrs. Sandwick had bought the books herself, one by one, out of her own meager salary. No wonder she wanted them taken care of!

She discovered the first week of school in September that I had a strong bent for spelling, and went out of her way in spelling bees to stump me—not to stump me, but to stretch me. And she did, all the way to the state championships, where I misspelled one of the few words she hadn't yet thrown at me. To this day I cannot read that word without seeing the look on her face when I missed it.

You've heard it so often that it's a cliché, but her library was an open window to a caged bird. There just weren't libraries accessible in those days to kids who lived in big cities. They were all downtown, miles away, gray stone mausoleums steeped in silence and forbidding to young would-be subscribers. But in the back of Mrs. Sandwick's room were all of Walter Farley, Albert Payson Terhune, and James Feni-more Cooper. There were Robert Louis Stevenson and Mark Twain. What a treasure chest!

And about the time I finished all of those, a new book appeared on the shelves, by someone I'd never heard of before—Charles Dickens. That was the beginning of a lifelong love affair, not only between me and Dickens, but between me and Mrs. Sand-wick, too, because I knew she'd bought it just for me. Three years later, when I graduated from the ninth grade, and we were never to see each other again, she gave it to me: "To Bill Lange, with Congratulations from Gertrude Sandwick, June 1950."

We hear a lot, in every age, about "the rising tide of mediocrity in education," and a lot about who or what is to blame. We have fretted from time to time about the Germans, or the Russians, or the Japanese getting ahead of us—whatever that means. We worry about losing our technological edge, and deplore the pressures that beset our kids from every side. In an age grown cautious and litigious, we snipe at those who would lead us and argue among our-selves which way wisdom and integrity lie. Increas-ingly, I think, we sense that this is not a golden age in the history of our republic.

I don't pretend to know any of the answers. But I have a hunch that they're much simpler than we think, and that they have more to do with the spirit in which we perform than the technology we use to do it. It's probably less important that I learned to multiply seven by eight than that Joey Gardner helped me learn it. It's certainly less important that I learned never to use *like* as a subordinate conjunction than that I became aware that language, just like music, must be mastered before it can be manipulated.

Those flash cards and grammar drills were the stern, gray tools that Mrs. Sandwick used to instill those enduring lessons. She taught us far more than we thought we could handle, and we learned that we could handle far more than we thought. After that, as far as she was concerned, she had done her best and we were on our own. But after that, we were ready for it. Not too bad for an old Ziegfeld Follies girl. This is the only way now that I can thank her.

# Kesselheim, You Creep!

LENNY KESSELHEIM, YOU CREEP! WHERE are you today? Wherever you are, do you know that you've been living for decades under a curse that I borrowed from the poet Don Marquis and pronounced on you?—i hope that [your] soul for a thousand turns of the wheel of existence bides in the shell of a louse dodging a fine-toothed comb.

For the last thirty years I've lived in a college town where there's a lot of coming and going—junior professors who don't make it, interns and residents who move on, retired alumni who stay a few years and move into managed care. And I never see the moving vans being loaded or unloaded, with the family standing around—parents, kids, dogs, cat cages—but I think again of Lenny the Creep. It was just about 55 years ago that he came into my life and, like a vandal in a vegetable garden, did his very best to make it as miserable as he could.

Life is full of traumas, great and small, for all of us; but one of the most incomprehensible to kids is that of moving. Uprooted from their familiar surroundings, for reasons often obscure, and lied to terribly by those they have trusted the most—"You're going to love it there."—they are then cast upon a strange and alien shore. Lucky are the few of them whose parents have the time and take the trouble, in their new situations, to help them adjust.

For normally the parents themselves are busy adjusting—to a new home, a new job, grossly altered circumstances—and the kids, like a litter of orphaned fox pups, are left to explore things themselves.

I sympathize. I remember quite clearly the summer of 1943. I hadn't known till then that the act of moving even existed, that it was a thing people actually did. But my father's new job predicated moving west from Albany to Syracuse. And suddenly we had done it. Not a very impressive distance—less than 150 miles. But from a familiar, urban, paved, brick-walled world filled and surrounded by stolid German-American parents, grandparents, aunts, uncles, great-aunts, and even great-grandmothers, we transferred suddenly to a world of single-family houses, lawns, and no relations. No Protestants, either; just Irish Catholics everywhere, in a neighborhood dominated by the twin steeples of Most Holy Rosary Church. I'd never been so alone before, or felt such an alien. Which is where you came in, Lenny, you troll.

One of the first things kids do when they reach their new homes is cock their ears and listen for the cries of other kids their ages. Rather like what the Starship Enterprise folks do when approaching an unfamiliar planet: check for intelligent life. Perceiving it, they then approach very cautiously and test the waters for signs of benevolence.

Which is exactly what I did. And was delighted to discover a whole tribe of humanoids whose ages bracketed mine, who spoke English (but only English, unlike many of the kids where I had come from), and who were quite friendly. I rejoiced, went home for my wagon, and joined a couple of them in rolling happily down Stinard Avenue hill.

That was your cue, I guess. For after a couple of days of playing with my new friends, I showed up the third day, and there you were. And it seemed that right from the start you were dedicated to raining on my parade, throwing a monkey wrench into my works, blighting the bloom on my rose. You were destiny's designated hitter, you degraded numskull.

You stood there listening for a couple of minutes. Big as you were, you were impossible to ignore. First thing you said after collecting your dim wits was, "Why do you call a cart a wagon? Is that what they call carts where you came from?" A little later you jumped on "carmallow," which was supposed to be "carmel." I found myself wishing I'd introduced myself as Bill, instead of Billy. When you said, "Billy," it sounded suddenly very dumb.

If I'd known then what I know now, I'd have given you a shot right on the end of the nose, with no warning, because that's where it was bound to end, anyway. Instead, I just blushed, and suffered what no kid in such an exposed, vulnerable position ought to have to endure: a lesson in being less than all right. I also know now why you did it. I sympathize, but it was still a shitty thing for you to do.

You made me aware of several other things I wouldn't have noticed, or at least have minded, without your help: that my family were indeed the only Protestants on the street; that my glasses were dumb-looking; that my parents were handicapped. What a sweetheart you were!

After you finally knocked me off my wagon and sat on me, contentedly pounding, I discovered some other stuff that I wouldn't have otherwise: that you were as slow of foot as of wit; that you could neither catch me nor conjure a quick riposte to any epithets delivered safely out of reach; and that, in those days of the Second World War, you absolutely hated being called "Herman German Kesselheim," and being reminded that your black eyebrows met in the middle. Sorry, pal, but we just brought out the worst in each other.

I think of you these days when I see moving vans, and pray that your seeds of malevolence might have proven infertile; that those kids, climbing out of cars with out-of-state plates, and gazing around them for the first time at their new homes, might never meet someone like you. But I know better. You, unfortunately, are as normal as measles.

On the other hand, you taught me something priceless: that none of us should ever pass a van unloading in our neighborhood without stopping to shake somebody's hand, say hello, and ask how we can help. That nobody should ever have to feel far from home where we have the power to help him. Thanks, you troglodyte, for crawling out from under your rock, sitting on my chest, and teaching me that. I hope it bothers you that, in your own unique way, you have helped make my world a better place to live. Herman . . . !

# The End of Mr. Auchincloss

A WARM LATE SEPTEMBER SUNDAY. WE had the windows of our dormitory room open to the afternoon sun, the *pock-pock* of tennis rackets, the shouts of a touch football game, and the aroma of wet fallen leaves. The record player was stacked with 45-rpm discs playing peppy *fin de siècle* overtures—Offenbach and Suppé. Stewart and I and a few other students were just sitting around on the beds and chairs, avoiding getting to work on our assignments for Monday, when we heard the crunch of tires in the gravel parking lot beside the dormitory.

Stewart got up to take a look. He started back in mock surprise, his eyes wide, flinging out his elbows. "Whoa!" he exclaimed. "Come take a look at this!"

It was a brand-new 1952 red Pontiac convertible with the top down. The back seat was piled up to the windowsills with the kind of stuff guys take to school with them—a floor lamp, a record player, a bookcase, and a few framed prints. The driver got out.

Big horn-rimmed glasses on a pink, sort of prissy face; black hair with a pompadour over the right temple; slender; dark blue blazer with brass buttons, buttondown shirt with a rep tie; gray slacks; and white bucks. I mean white bucks. We all wore them then, but nobody ever cleaned them. As soon as we bought a new pair, we walked all over them to get them dirty. This guy obviously had bought one of those talcum powder-filled bags and whitened his bucks. Sons of the middle class that we were, we disliked him on sight.

After a couple of years' attendance at any preparatory school, any half-alert student gets to know the lay of the land intimately. In the seething, tension-laden equilibrium between boisterous battalions of pubescent males and grim-faced patrols of faculty members, you soon learn what you can get away with, and what you can't, and with whom; who springs pop quizzes on Monday mornings; which faculty wives are the nicest, which the best-looking, and which those who scream at their husbands. Everything gets ironed out and runs along more or less smoothly, as long as nobody pushes or pulls too hard in an unacceptable direction. Tradition and homogeneity are in themselves virtues of the first order. To stick out is to be a sore thumb.

Somehow Mr. Auchincloss had not figured that out before he arrived. And as far as I can tell, he never did. He'd come to replace a very nice guy, a French master who'd suffered a ruptured appendix and taken the year off. But in a red convertible and white bucks? Not bright.

I roomed with my chum Stewart in a corner double beside the stairs on the first floor of the dorm. Everybody coming in and going out had to pass our door. Directly above us was the empty apartment of the master who'd had to leave. This is where the new guy was headed. And directly above that apartment lived probably the world's unlikeliest pair of roommates, but also its greatest and most underrated comedy tag team: Roscoe Stinson, III, and Cyrus Appleby.

Roscoe was very quick; Cyrus was very slow. Roscoe spoke rapidly, like H. V. Kaltenborn, with his teeth held together; Cyrus spoke very little, but breathed adenoidally through his mouth, his jaw hanging slack. Roscoe was perpetually brimming with outrageous, potentially felonious ideas; and Cyrus was just dumb enough to want to give them a try.

The white bucks passed our door, climbed the stairs, and entered the new digs. The floors in the dorm were concrete; we could hear every sound. He opened the windows, came back down in his shirt-sleeves, and lugged his stuff in. He put up the top on his convertible, closed the windows, and locked the doors—unheard of on that quiet campus. Then he went back up and closed his door, and we could hear him putting everything away.

The first week passed quietly. We nodded if we passed him in the hall—"Good morning." We checked the name tag on his door—Mr. Auchin-closs. We made as little noise as possible, listening, learning his habits. He seemed to study when we did, during study hall in the evening, but never went to breakfast. He opened the windows of his car slightly on sunny days, but didn't use it.

Then he made his first move, and it was a horrible strategic error. He'd no doubt been listening to faculty chatter about the ambiance of dormitory life. But instead of waiting to confirm it by his own experience, he must have decided on preemption.

Saturday afternoon. We had been neighbors for

just six days. Stewart was studying, and I was about to leave for a cross-country meet. We heard Mr. Auchincloss's chair scrape on the floor above; his door opened, he pattered down the stairs, and knocked on our door. Instant attention. Stewart raised his eyebrows, got up, and opened the door.

"Hello, fellows," he said.

"Sir," we responded as one.

"If you have a minute, there are a couple of things I'd like to discuss with you." His voice rose in pitch, almost to a falsetto. We waited, expectant and delighted.

"It has come to my attention, in discussions with other faculty members, that you young men sometimes have . . . that is, you hold . . . oh, I think they call them singalongs, after church on Sundays, and you play guitars and ukuleles and sing folk songs. Well, as you know, Sunday is a day of rest and quiet in the dormitories; and in addition, I will be studying or entertaining guests in my rooms from time to time on the weekends. So you will have to find somewhere else to sing your little songs." Little songs? Stewart and I were stunned. Protest was the nearest thing to our lips. But this was too good to interrupt. We held our silence as he continued.

"Furthermore," he went on, his voice sounding now almost like Sarah Vaughan, "I've been told that you boys"—now we were boys—"that you boys occasionally have . . . have . . . oh, I can hardly bring myself to say it? From time to time you have ghastly, awful belching and farting contests down here!" Somebody had spilled the beans, as it were.

He was squeaking with outrage. "There's no use to

deny it. I refuse to talk about it, it's so beneath the level of acceptable behavior. I will say only that, as of now, it has stopped!"

We nodded together. "Yes, sir," we said. I glanced over at Stewart's face. To someone who didn't know him, it was impassive. To someone who did, it said, "You are dead meat!"

We held off for about three weeks, and I'm sure he thought we were duly cowed. And then one Sunday afternoon, when we knew he was studying, we started. Guitar and a couple of soup spoons. We warmed up with "The Wabash Cannonball," and the guys in the next rooms came in to join us. They knew what was afoot. "Old Shep," "Blue Eyes Cryin' in the Rain"—all classics. We ignored Mr. Auchincloss's rapping on the radiator. Finally his chair squeaked, his door banged, and he came downstairs to shut us up.

Our room was still, pregnant with anticipation. Two minutes passed. Then Roscoe began, up on the third floor. Sitting at his desk, he dropped a ping-pong ball onto the floor, let it bounce four times, and grabbed it. He waited exactly fifteen seconds and repeated the operation—over and over at fifteen-second intervals. Then, maddeningly, he broke the sequence for about a minute and began again. The sound was barely audible, but it was absolutely irresistible. We could literally feel Mr. Auchincloss listening. But he couldn't tell what it was.

Roscoe's operation was exquisite. Every evening after that, during study hall, he'd wait till exactly 8:30 and start it. Mr. Auchincloss could stand it for about five minutes. Then the chair scraped, his door flew open, and up the stairs he went.

Bang, bang, bang, bang on the door, and without waiting for an answer, swinging it open. Roscoe and Cyrus at their desks. "What is that infernal noise?"

"Noise, sir? What noise? I don't hear anything. Do you hear a noise, Cyrus?"

"Huh? Nope, I don't hear no noise."

Back down the stairs, two flights. Bang, bang on our door, his red face and horn rims poking into the room. Stewart and I, absorbed in our studies, looked up from our textbooks. Same routine as upstairs: we shook our heads soberly, listening intently. His voice was cracking. You could tell the rest of him wasn't far behind.

On the climactic night, Roscoe was superb. He absolutely outdid himself, alternating regular sequences with maddeningly irregular interruptions. Even Stewart and I, two floors below, were going nuts. Then, after almost half an hour of tap-tap-tap-tap, a window somewhere in the dorm shot open. Somebody stuck his head outside and began to make retching, and then vomiting noises. Mr. Auchincloss's chair screaked, his window opened, too, and he stuck his head out, demanding, "Who is that boy?"

Cyrus was generally incapable of taking what is called the long view. The three-week wait for this moment had been almost more than he could bear. His student job was garbage man up at the dining hall, and several days before this he'd brought back to the dorm a pot of spoiled clam chowder that had ever since been quietly seasoning and reeking in his clothes closet. During study hall, he'd been in the third-floor bathroom, heating a balloon full of the chowder in a sink full of warm water. Now, as Mr. Auchincloss's head appeared beneath him, protruding into the brisk November night, he finally realized his destiny.

Stewart looked at the window with an expression of almost spiritual rapture. "By god!" he said, as the grisly mess streamed past, "I think that struck something on the way down."

# A Carpenter in Indian Summer

ABOUT 9:30 I TAKE A TEN-MINUTE BREAK, sliding a saw horse over into the sun. The coffee steams as I pour it out into the little green plastic cup. I unwrap a piece of corn bread and, lacking a steamer or toaster, lay it down over the top of the coffee cup to warm up a little. Old Jasper, an ancient gray tiger, has been sitting in the sunny doorway as I worked. Now, hearing the rustle of waxed paper, he comes picking his way through the sawdust and rubs against my ankles. I set a crumb of corn bread on a wooden shingle down beside my feet. He sniffs at it gingerly and spurns it, looking up: that all you got?

When you consider that there are millions of people who can't find work, you've got to deem it a blessing to have all you can do. When over the years you discover that you like what you do—maybe even love it—that's a blessing, too. And when you work most of the time out of doors and get the kind of weather we've had so far this fall—well, all of that is more than anybody could possibly deserve.

High above my head, studs, headers, and rafters are etched against the sky in a logical and graceful geometry. Each piece clasps a few others in mutual support, each helping all the others to do their particular jobs. Soon they'll be covered up in plywood and plaster. They'll disappear from sight until long years after I've done the same. This is when a building is most beautiful to me, when the bones of it are being assembled, and it seems a shame to cover them up.

Wood is alive. When you spend a great deal of time with it, you discover that it has as much personality as people. I talked to a steelworker once who said that his steel did, too; but I doubted that. Steel was never alive, and any character it has was created by its manufacturer. Each piece of wood, though, whispers its autobiography to you as you pick it up, weigh it half-consciously in your hands, squint along it for straightness, and locate the knots and imperfections that may give you trouble.

I'm amazed, for example, at how many eight-foot-long Canadian two-by-fours I pick up that have heart wood in their end grain. They must be cutting some pretty small sticks indeed up in Québec. I feel the way German generals must have felt in 1945, trying to fight the war with adolescent soldiers.

There's been a shower during the night, and the house is redolent of wet wood. There's the sour smell of the pressure-treated southern yellow pine sills; the heavy odor of Canadian spruce and western fir; the stench of poplar sheathing like cheap perfume; and strongest of all, the sweet aroma of white cedar. It smells like a clothes closet, or a dog bed.

I remember the moment all this began. I was twenty years old, living in a small village in the Adirondacks, out of college, and out of a job. Somebody down at the dinette mentioned that a contractor named Harvey Branch was looking for help. I went right down.

Harvey was a cheerful little man with a perpetually optimistic attitude. I think he got that way from the necessity of raising his head to talk with almost everyone he met, of having to look up. He also had a very casual approach to the use of consonants: whenever you asked him how things were going, he always answered, "Oh, boy! Fings are wookin' up, wookin' up!"

I presented myself: tall, skinny, unknown, and bearded—in a time when beards were not yet fashionable; *On the Road* was in its first flush of success. "Ya wookin' fa wuk, eh?" said Harvey. "Know anyfing 'bout coppentwy?" Well, I had a hammer and a handsaw in the trunk of my old Plymouth, so I said yes. We settled on $1.35 an hour to start, and he sent me off to look up Gussie Edmonds, the foreman on one of his construction jobs.

Gussie had the sour, brown face of a terminal dyspeptic and a skeptical cast in his eye. He looked me up and down, handed me a ten-foot straightedge and a bundle of wood shingles, and set me to work shimming furring strips in a wall about to be paneled. Forty-five minutes later he took a look at my work and fired me. "Go back to the office and pick up your time," he said, clearly pleased that his first impression had been confirmed.

But as luck would have it, just as I was explaining to Harvey what had happened, in walked an elderly man in a Pendleton shirt, wool pants, and a brown fedora with a small copper shield pinned to it—a New York State guide's license. "Harvey," he began. "By god, I hope you can help me out. I need a man to help me up t' the lakes."

Harvey raised his chin as he always did when thinking, and our eyes met. "By gowwy!" he exclaimed. "I got just the man!"

You couldn't pay enough money to get a job as wonderful as that one. I spent the next couple of months in a log cabin camp way back in the woods, hauling lumber and building materials from the end of the road to the job, traveling through some of the most beautifully preserved forest in the East. It was all muscle power—a guide boat for two miles up a lower lake, another mile with an old-fashioned one-wheel L.L. Bean deer carrier, and then another guide boat up a second lake to the camp. I dug holes for concrete footings in ground that was—as one of the old guys in camp said—"'most two rocks to ever' dirt," with black flies wallowing in the sweat, citronella, and pine tar on my neck and arms. I stained lumber with a mixture of creosote and diesel fuel that burned little circles wherever it splashed on bare skin. I mixed concrete and mortar and tarred leaky roofs. And I listened and watched as two of the best carpenters who ever lived, Bill Broe and Jim Brown, put up a big log building as tight and true and lovely as a Stradivarius.

They argued about almost everything—how deep to bury water lines; which way to swing a door; where to put the hot water heater. Each of them wanted to do everything we did in the best possible way. But there was clearly more than one best possible way. Listening to them, I soaked up more than in any college course I ever took: mostly that, techniques and skills aside, there were values and ethics involved in the work of carpenters as much as in that of priests and politicians.

Old George Lamb was our cook. He spent most of every day simmering pot roasts and baking pies, cornbread, and cookies down in the kitchen building. He had a gift for pancakes that I've never seen equaled by anyone else. I can remember eating over two dozen of them at breakfast without any distress, stopping only because the batter was gone. His rice pudding was ambrosial; Jim and I complained, every time he made it, that he hadn't made enough. So in a final spasm, he used up all the sugar in camp and made the pudding in a porcelain dish pan. "There, goddam yez!" he cried as he banged it down onto the oilcloth table top, "Eat that!" And we did, for a very long time.

After supper in the cool, loon-calling spring evenings, we sat around the kitchen, and the three old men told stories. It wasn't intentional on their part; they were just talking. The comedies and tragedies of life in a mountain village ran through every tale, and I don't think I've forgotten a single word they spoke. If I ever have a choice of heaven, that'll be it.

Well, that was over forty years ago now, and all those old guys have gone to their rewards, which I hope are great. I still visit them now and then, but it's in the Sand Hill Cemetery, with its incredible view of the Great Range to the southwest. The lakes and the camps where we worked together are still there, but to me will never be the same without them.

The 9:30 break is still the same, though: the morning sun just warming to its task, the aroma of wood and shavings, the shrieking of blue jays back in the woods. The throb of a finger where a cedar splinter has got to come out at lunchtime. I can hear old Bill—and a dozen other old-timers I've worked with over the years—as if he were still sitting next to me, snapping his lunch pail shut and signaling the end of the break with his unvarying, "Way-ull . . . "

I shake the last cool drops of coffee from the green cup and screw it back onto its thermos. There can't be too many creatures happier than a carpenter in Indian summer.

# Foozie

I READ WOMEN'S MAGAZINES NOW AND then, for the same reason people climb Mount Everest: because they are there. In the bathroom. My wife is forever carting the decent magazines back out to the coffee table in the living room.

As a result, I probably know more than the average man does about raising begonias, getting rid of cellulitis, and choosing a sensitive, caring remodeling contractor. But most of all, I know about marriages—what's wrong with them, whether they can (or should) be saved, where good people went wrong, what couples fight about, and how to patch up a botched union, once you've decided it's worth it. The Library of Congress, Masters and Johnson, and Dr. Ruth all together have nothing on me.

The other morning I got some bad news. About the time Mother was finishing her first cup of coffee, I was taking one of those multiple-choice rate-your-marriage tests. To my chagrin, I discovered that we're incompatible and probably aren't going to make it. I went out to the kitchen and broke it to her as gently as possible.

"According to this article here, my treasure, our relationship is doomed, and we're headed for some real terminal trouble unless we alter some of our, uh

. . . here it is—our 'techniques for accommodating each other's need for spatial autonomy.'"

"Uh, huh," she said. She was dividing her attention between Katie Couric and *Kitchen and Bath Ideas.*

"Don't you care about that? "

"Sure I do. I took the same test, and they're right: the odds are against us. But we knew that forty years ago. Remember what the priest told us? There's nothing that hasn't happened to us yet that could part us. Except death, maybe. Other than that, nothing."

"Nothing? How can you be so sure?" I persisted.

"Because anytime I get thinking I just can't stand it anymore, I remember that first apartment. I remember Foozie. Nothing seems hard after that."

Foozie! How could I have forgotten her? That fierce mongoose of a woman who, like a blue-hot cutting torch, tried to sear my new wife and me out of our first apartment and succeeded instead only in brazing us more firmly together.

That really was her name, too; at least that's what everybody called her. I never heard any other. She'd been a Gravelle before she married Poor Paul Leblanc. About five feet high, maybe 105 pounds soaking wet, blue eyes like ice and an ash-blond ponytail, she had the face of one of those pensive angels you see in stained glass depictions of the burial of Christ. And the personality of a rabid ferret.

Not to mention the vocabulary of a logger. She had a gift that I have envied for four decades: of stringing together individual, apparently unrelated

Anglo-Saxon epithets in a series that, coming from her, made sense. There is no way I can even suggest the incredible color of her conversation.

She and her husband (a pleasant, bumbling, beery day laborer whose glasses slid down to the tip of his nose after two bottles of beer and whom everyone called Poor Paul) and their three beautiful little blond girls lived on the first floor of a two-apartment building that, if it had been built properly in the first place, could have seen better days. I lived on the second floor. Every move I made upstairs made a noise downstairs; every oath she uttered downstairs made me cringe upstairs. And for a septic system we shared a 55-gallon drum full of rocks out in the back yard. My sewage had the drop on hers, so to speak, so some difficulties were inevitable. She washed her kids' diapers in her kitchen sink and rinsed them in her bathtub. If I flushed my toilet upstairs during the rinse cycle, the plug popped out of her tub and . . . well, you get the picture.

In addition, she used her railed-in front porch as a playpen for her girls and a shelter for her washline. I used mine, just above, as a daytime pen for my half-mad beagle, Frank. The porch floor leaked; so, unfortunately, did Frank. I did the best I could to spread newspapers for him, but to little effect. I couldn't get used to the sight of Foozie standing out in the road at the edge of the yard, shaking her fist up at my porch and screaming maledictions at me and Frank. So as soon as I could, I traded Frank for a cheap fly rod. But the damage was done, the breach between us irreparable. Her little girls, the oldest of them only five, always greeted me, when I came home from work. "Hi, Goddam Willy Lange! They thought that was my name.

Paul and I worked together in the woods, and took turns driving. He was somehow never eager to return home at the end of the day, and I came to dread the daily suggestion, "Let's stop at the Elm Tree for a quick one." Within half an hour his glasses were sliding down his nose, and he was hunting through his pockets for his car keys. Paul wasn't that great a driver stone sober. But have you ever tried to take the keys away from a French logger? If I was driving, he let himself slide into semi-consciousness before I could get him out of there. By the time we arrived home, he was fast asleep. Foozie could hear me fumbling at her storm door latch with one hand while dragging Paul with the other, and she always yanked the inside door open. If Paul betrayed any signs of awareness, she fired only one barrel; if he pretended sleep, she fired both, and I got my share.

Into this scene of domestic bliss I brought my new wife, a gentle and genteel product of a young ladies' college in the Shenandoah Valley. Frank was long gone by then, but Foozie was still in a stew. About a month earlier, during hunting season, I'd shot a buck. To cool the carcass and keep it up out of the reach of neighborhood dogs, I'd hung it from the ceiling of my porch to cure for a couple of days. But it had been still dripping. It had taken over where Frank had left off; but these stains were indelible.

As we moved my bride's luggage into the apartment, I deliberately did not stop downstairs and introduce her to Foozie. It just seemed easier that way. With Foozie, the end of every engagement was the same, so you deferred it as long as possible. I showed my bride how to operate the space heater in the living room, and which kerosene drum under the back stairs was ours. I demonstrated the proper techniques for lighting the gas hot water heater and the cranky gas oven. I showed her the marks on the floor indicating where to put the sap buckets when it rained or snowed. Then, like Bluebeard, I cautioned her, "Never, never flush the toilet or drain the tub when you hear water running downstairs!"

I guess I knew she'd forget; but I also knew she'd forget only once. I came home from work about a week later, carried Paul inside downstairs, and went upstairs, to find her in tears, huddled on the bed in a corner. "She ran right out into the middle of the road!" she sobbed. "And she shook her fist up here and screamed so all the neighbors could hear her. And you can't imagine what she said!"

Oh, yes, I could. And ever since, whenever we're having a particularly bad day, and I entertain that black thought, "I've had it. That's it!" I have only to recall the picture of my bride and me cowering in our living room as we heard Foozie downstairs discovering her tub backing up again. And after that, anything else seems like a summer shower. Till we are parted by death, my dear. I don't care what the tests say!

# Advice from Mr. Frost

IT WAS MAY OF 1962, AND THE OHIO
spring was in full bloom—fields turning green,
Amishmen in shirtsleeves driving their black bug-
gies, and cardinals singing from the forsythia bushes.
After nine years of desultory attendance punctuated
by many adventures, including marriage, I was finally closing in upon graduation from the College of
Wooster. And my wife and I, on the fifteenth of the
month, celebrated the arrival of our second child, a
son.

Besides attending classes and studying minimally,
I worked evenings at the Wooster Bus Station. I sold
tickets, checked and carried baggage, cleaned the
men's room, announced arrivals and departures of
Greyhound and Trailways buses, answered the
phone, and planned itineraries.

The owner of the station, its snack bar, and the
Wooster Cab Company was a rotund and fairly
pleasant local-boy-made-good named Marvin. Marvin dressed almost always in dark polyester suit and
tie, treated his customers cordially, and drove a black
Cadillac. He also was carrying on an affair with
Marsha, the woman who ran the snack bar for him
and dispatched taxicabs during the day. The two of
them disappeared regularly each evening at the end

of her shift. It fell to me to take calls from Marvin's wife when she was looking for him. "He's stepped out," I would respond—Marvin made this easy for me by never sharing anything—"and I expect him back. When he comes in, I'll have him call you." Marvin's end of this tacit bargain was to make the call when I gave him the message.

The College of Wooster was in a bit of a stew that spring. The president, Howard Lowry, was a former Princeton English professor and a personal friend of Robert Frost. Frost was becoming quite old and feeble, but Dr. Lowry had invited him to give the commencement address. Frost had been ill, and had declined; so the president went with his second choice, Henry Luce. Then, as Commencement approached, Frost revived and decided he could make it, after all. What to do? You don't tell Henry Luce that your first choice has replaced him. But by great good fortune, Wooster was also dedicating a new library that same week. So Frost was invited to give an address in honor of the new building.

I'd been devoted to Frost for years, beginning in 1953, when our senior English master at prep school had taken several of us to Amherst to listen to him read his poetry. From that time on, if he was speaking anywhere nearby and I could get there, I went. I read and memorized great chunks of my favorite Frost poems. So, even though it occurred two days after our son was born, I was on hand for his reading at Wooster. His death was only months away; it would be the last time I was to see him at a podium.

Late in the morning Frost held a news conference on the slate-floored, covered piazza at the east end of the president's house. Of course I was there. Frost sat in a comfortable chair on the edge of the piazza, his liver-spotted skin dark and his white hair gleaming in the sun, and fielded the questions of the eager local journalists. He was clearly exhausted. I stood at the outer edge of the ring and listened. I'd been associated with the college almost as long as Dr. Lowry, and we knew each other well. Both of us, underneath everything else, were aspiring writers. He spotted me and gave me a high sign.

The questions were mostly mundane and predictable: How did you get into poetry? What's poetry have that prose doesn't? How did you settle on New England as the scene of most of your work? But then it suddenly got more exciting.

"Haven't I read somewhere," began a bright-eyed young woman reporter, "that you're the poet laureate of the United States?"

"Yes, that's true," he answered.

"Is that a paying position?"

"I serve," he responded dryly with a hint of a smile, "without emolument."

"That's nice," she pursued. "But do you get paid for it?"

"There is no emolument connected with the honor," he said—a trifle testily, I thought.

"Yes, but what's the salary?" she insisted. You could feel some people beginning to edge away from the imminent explosion.

"Young lady," he said. "Your business is supposed to be words. I suggest you go back to your office, get a dictionary, and look up 'emolument.' Then, if you want to, come back and ask me some more questions."

Dr. Lowry stole around the outside of the circle, sidled up to me and asked, "Would you be willing to show Mr. Frost around the campus this afternoon after his address, and then this evening come with us when we take him back to his hotel in Cleveland?" Would I! "You can bring him back here around four; and then come at seven, and we'll go to Cleveland." He slipped onto the piazza behind Frost and signaled that everybody should beat it.

I went to visit my wife and brand-new son at the hospital, told her about the chance to go to Cleveland with Mr. Frost in the college limousine, and went home to call Marvin.

"Marvin," I said, "I've got to take this evening off. I've got a once-in-a-lifetime opportunity, and I just won't be able to make it." I told him what I'd been invited to do. But I don't think he knew Robert Frost from Melvil Dewey.

"I need you this evening," he answered. "Marsha and I are going over the books together tonight." My heart sank. Going over the books, my ass! But I knew there was no point in arguing with him. There's no cerebral tissue in the pelvic girdle, and, anyway, Marvin wasn't used to not getting what he wanted.

"Well, I'm sorry, Marvin, but I need to do this. I'll never get a chance like this again."

"You do whatever you need to do, then. I'm just going to have to try to find somebody a little more reliable, I guess."

"I'm really sorry about that," I said. I meant it, too;

I had a wife and two kids now, and I needed that job. "But I can't pass this up. I'll call you tomorrow."

Frost had spent the noon hour autographing books over at the president's house—no paperbacks, we were told; he wouldn't sign them. Anybody who wanted an autograph left his book there, in a huge pile, with his name on a slip of paper in the flyleaf. Naturally, I left my *Complete Poems of Robert Frost,* which my bride had given me for Christmas a couple of years earlier.

The college chapel was jammed for Frost's reading. I stood leaning against a post at the head of the left-hand aisle, and watched him in profile as he "said" his poems and commented about what might or might not be concealed within them. There was nothing there, he said, decrying the analysts who said they had "vivisected" them for hidden implications. "You can't vivisect a poem," he said, "because the operation kills it. If I wanted a meaning there, I put it there."

During the question-and-answer period, someone asked how it felt to be so old, to be one of the last surviving giants of his generation. "It feels terrible," he answered. "All my friends have died, and I have conversation now only with younger people. It's very lonely." He had been leaning forward and supporting himself on the lectern with his elbows; and as he said this, he seemed to slump and lean even more heavily. President Lowry stood and, holding up the palms of his hands to forestall any more questions, thanked Frost for having come. Long standing ovation.

I met him at the vestry door a few minutes later,

and we strolled very slowly for a while around Wooster's brick campus—red brick walks underfoot, yellow brick and sandstone everywhere above ground level. Pure Ohio. In his lifetime, Frost had walked hundreds of campuses. I wondered if this one made him feel (as it did me) a long way from home in New England. He was easy to spot from a distance, of course, and people who saw him came hustling up to say hello, shake his hand, and tell him how much they adored his poetry. The old man was already a national monument. When he saw them coming, he stopped, and as they arrived, wearily held out both his hands to be shaken and nodded his head in acknowledgement of the expected praise.

After what seemed only a few minutes, I dropped him off at the president's house, found my Beetle, and drove up to the hospital to see my wife and our new son. Then back home for a quick supper with our daughter and her baby sitter. Finally, after a shower and lots of talcum—the evening was hot and oppressive—I put on my brand-new summer suit, a tie, and my good shoes and drove back to the president's house, arriving at seven on the button.

Doctor Lowry was there in the foyer, along with a couple of beautiful young women who had some kinship to either him or Frost, I don't know which. It didn't matter; the president was a bachelor, and surrounded himself with attractive women the way some people put vases full of flowers around the house. Frost wasn't there yet; still upstairs, we were told. But there were some books of his on the settee, books that he'd signed but that hadn't been picked up. I looked through them till I found mine, opened to the flyleaf, and discovered to my horror that he'd missed it.

A couple of minutes later we heard a shuffling in the upstairs hall, and here came the old man, dragging his own big Samsonite suitcase down the stairs. The president and I rushed to his aid, but he waved us off. "I can get it myself. I got it this far." How often since then have I heard those exact words in northern New England!

"Well, then," said Doctor Lowry, "if we're all ready . . . "

"Excuse me, sir," I said. "But my book . . . Mr. Frost, I left my book here, but I think you must have missed it."

"Let me see it." I opened to the flyleaf. "Have you got a pen?" I handed him mine. He set the book on an end table, bent over it, and read what was already there: *To my husband Will—Love Ida—Christmas 1960.* He turned his head toward me. "What's your name?" I told him.

He wrote laboriously, straining to see and to hold his hand steady: *To Will Lange from his friend Robert Frost, Andrews Library Day 1962.* "There!" he said. "That 'friend' business will make it worth a couple hundred dollars more after I'm gone." I don't think he had any inkling how much more it made it worth to me. (Years later, by the way, I discovered that he had signed the book already, but under his photograph opposite the title page. I hadn't thought to look there; one of the few times I've profited from an oversight.)

The four of us walked out the front door, where the College limousine was waiting: a 1957 Desoto four-door sedan, driven by the College chauffeur, a lively plumber from Buildings and Grounds named Lew Noletti. Lew bowed, saluted, and deferentially stowed Mr. Frost's suitcase in the trunk. Doctor Lowry arranged us for the ride. "I'll sit in the back between the ladies, and Will, you sit up front between Lew and Mr. Frost." I slipped into a state of quiet rapture. I'm sure it showed.

We climbed in, shut the doors, and cranked the windows down. No air conditioning in those days. Frost was clearly suffering from the heat. He reached up, pulled off his tie, and stuck it into his jacket pocket. Lew saw him do it, and did the same. So I did, too. Then Frost, suffering also from his sumptuous supper, reached down, undid his trousers, and unzipped his fly. Then—I couldn't believe it!—so did Lew! I sat there goggling back and forth at the two of them, thought, "No way!" crossed my wrists demurely in my lap, and looked straight ahead.

As we headed north out of Wooster toward Cleveland, Frost asked if I read much poetry. Yes, I told him, quite a bit. I wanted to be a poet myself someday. You'd better have a regular job, too, he cautioned, not realizing I'd just given up a regular job just to spend a few hours with him. Which poets did I like best? The two Roberts, Frost and Service, Walt Whitman, Don Marquis, Edna Millay, Emily Dickinson, and Edward Lear. He seemed pleased with the list. Did I have any favorites among his poems? Yes: *Mending Wall; After Apple-Picking;* and *'Out, Out—'* Why in the world *'Out, Out—'*? Well, I answered, it was easy to memorize. A faint little smile slightly deepened the heavy wrinkles around his habitually pursed mouth.

We passed the hospital where my wife and our infant son were spending the evening together. He noticed the hospital (seemed, in fact, to notice almost everything). "Doctor Lowry tells me you and your wife have just had a son."

"Yes, sir. Just a couple of nights ago."

"Isn't that wonderful. What are you going to name him?"

"Well, sir, in honor of your visit, we're thinking of calling him Robert Frost."

He half turned toward me. "Oh, no," he said, "that's not a good idea. You never name a child for anyone famous or notorious. It's not fair to the child. He spends his whole life trying either to live up to the name or to live it down. Haven't you any alternatives?"

"Yes, there's the family name, and I know the family would like that."

"What's that?"

Cringing inwardly, I murmured, "Willem Maurits Lange, the Fourth."

The old Desoto rolled through the long summer sunset at a smooth fifty miles an hour, north on Ohio Route 83. The little glacial hills rose and fell ahead of it like the bumps in a children's roller coaster; the green cornfields stretched toward knee-high; occasional oil well pumps bobbed up and down like great, long-legged birds drinking. Frost sat quietly, ruminating.

Finally he said, straight ahead at the windshield, "You better call him Robert Frost."

About an hour later I had my last look at the old man, forever. He was dragging his suitcase with one

hand through the glass doors of the Mark Hopkins
Hotel, and trying to wrap his crumpled tie around
his neck with the other.

# Notes from Mary O

*Dear Mrs. L—Got done vacumming and cloths early so worked out in front on garden some. Petunias and everthing gone to seed and dried up, so cleaned up hole garden and put stuff on cumpost pile out back. Ready for spring now. See you tommorow. Mary O*

That was the first note my wife ever got from Mary O'Connor, about forty years ago, as Mary prepared to leave after her first day of work in our house. It described her unwitting and total destruction of our prized little herb garden—lemon thyme, peppermint, rosemary, "everthing." It also marked the official beginning of a reign of terror unparalleled since the days of the Scythians.

My wife and I were both teaching, but in different schools. Our younger kid was in morning kindergarten. Neither of us could ever get home before 3:30 in the afternoon. So we needed an afternoon babysitter who'd do a little housework.

*Dear Mrs. L—Forgot the coco on the stove today while arning. Pot burnt, plastic handel melted. Dont like plastic handeld pots anyway. Get some with metal ones. All my other ladys have them and like them alot.*

44

It was quite a job to find a cleaning lady in town. We asked all around, but every woman who did cleaning was already booked up. Then we heard that Mary O'Connor might be available. She ran a little snack bar down by the summer colony from Memorial Day to Labor Day, and might be looking for winter work. Nobody we talked to had ever employed her, or known anybody else who had, but they all mentioned her energy and honesty. We talked to her, and were impressed by her cheerfulness and enthusiasm. She would have to bring her little boy, Bunchy, with her, she said. That was fine with us. We hired her for three hours each weekday afternoon.

I'll tell you, if John Kennedy had hired Mary, as we did, in 1963, for the same hours each afternoon as we did, and shipped her to Viet Nam, the war would have ended quite differently.

*Dear Mrs. L—My little boy Bunchy shore does like your cat. He was folowing her around the kitchen today and catch his toe on the arning cord. Thats it for the arn. But all my other ladies nowdays have perm. press clothes anyway and I think you out to try them too.*

Mary, her surname notwithstanding, was not Irish. Her father had come down from Sherbrooke in the '30s to work in the local paper mill. She was about five feet tall, stocky and muscular, with a close-cropped cap of black curls and more pure animal energy than anyone else I've ever met. But she had a spectacular lack of two things: self-doubt and a rear-view mirror.

*Dear Mrs. L—Took plastic cups out of bath today and*

*got rid of them, they colect germs. Glass not good in bath.*
*Will bring paper cups next time.*

Mary's husband, Elton, ran a Sunoco garage with
doors high enough for log trucks, so they were the
bulk of his business. He wasn't quite the ball of fire
that Mary was, but he looked and acted like a very
tough cookie. He'd have had to be, to wade through
the swath of destruction that Mary left behind. I
watched him cure himself of an infected thumb one
day by heating the end of a welding rod with an
acetylene torch and burning through the thumbnail.
There were three or four of us watching him. When
the smoke and steam began to rise, we all suddenly
had business somewhere else.

*Dear Mrs. L—The shower curten had some of the*
*ring holes tore out so got rid of it. Am going up to St J this*
*weekend if you want me to get you one. I know Will likes*
*shower. Tell him to take baths til new one gets put up.*

She was starting to drive us crazy. We were afraid
to come home afternoons for fear of what we'd
find—or rather, what we wouldn't find. But we were
both pretty young and inexperienced, lacking the
self-confidence to tell her that it just wasn't working
out. We tried locking up or hiding things we didn't
want destroyed or discarded, but that didn't help at
all. She struck like lightning and tornadoes, haphaz-
ardly and unpredictably.

*Dear Mrs. L—Found these real pretty glasses in the*
*cubbard with the ducks on them, all dusty so washed*

46

*them. Gave Bunchy a drink and he droped it, sorry theres
only 5 now. No harm done cause you dont use them much
anyway. Ate that old peice of apple pie in refrig. Hope
you wernt saving it shore was good.*

We were getting desperate, and going broke in the
bargain. Plus which, we were getting little hints from
our son (who has always preferred death to snitch-
ing) that Bunchy was dismantling his toys and beat-
ing him with the pieces. Bunchy was a year older and
much larger than our son, and repeating kindergarten. He suffered from hip dysplasia, and wore an
A-shaped plaster cast on both legs that held his feet
permanently about twenty inches apart. He ambu-
lated by planting his crutches and swinging his feet
forward. And with those feet and one crutch planted, he could swing the other crutch in a pretty deadly
arc. He'd inherited his father's toughness and insen-
sitivity, so there wasn't much hope that our kid would
suddenly rise up and turn the tables.

We racked our brains. There had to be some
way—short of one of us quitting his job, or deeply
offending her—to get rid of poor, sunny Mary. She
was demolishing our home and peace of mind.
Where she really belonged was out in the woods with
Elton's customers, loading logs and pulpwood. We
made lists of reasons she might find plausible, and
rehearsed scenarios, but none of them would do the
trick. They were all transparent and, when people
asked her—as they surely would—why she'd "got
done up at the teacher's," would cause her to lose
face. In desperation, we finally prayed together for
deliverance.

Never doubt the efficacy of prayer. In mid-January my wife was suddenly transferred to a central school with an all-day kindergarten, and they said she could take our son with her!

We put it to him. "Would you like to change to a brand-new school with kindergarten all day . . . " we began. His face clouded. " . . . and not come home every day to stay with Mary and Bunchy?" A radiant smile suffused his ruddy little face. The reign of terror was over!

But Mary had one last great effort left in her. It was her valedictory, and I have treasured it all these years. She wrote it in chapters during the course of her last afternoon.

*Dear Mrs. L—Brought a suprise for my last day 3 squirrels Elton shot put in oven for supper. Should be ready at about 6. Oven therm reads low you need electric stove. Vacummed soot and ashes out of fireplace you need more vacumm bags. Found old cabbage stew in refrig. had Bunchy flush it down john. John wudnt take it overflowed, think you have roots in sooerline. Your vacumm doesn't vacumm up water, most of my ladys does. Vacumm bag broke from water, soot come out back end. Wanted to wash soot out of drapes and bedspreds ect. but couldnt cause sooerline plugged. You need snake will take stuff home to wash, bring back Wensday. Oven therm isnt low, squirrels burnt. Close upstairs windows when you get home, smoke should be out by then. Will bring some more when Elton goes again. Hope Billy likes his new school. Bunchy and I shore will miss him. Bye for now. Mary O*

# Christmas on the Party Line

I WAS FILLING OUT A MEDICARE FORM the other day, and it struck me how much things have changed around me, even though I haven't— not all that much, anyway. I've had the same name now for over sixty years. And this town has even fewer people in it now than when I was young. But my address has gotten a lot more complicated— Highway Contract number, box number, zip code. And my telephone number! Takes half a minute just to dial all the numbers! That's if you can remember 'em all, without checking halfway through to see if you're still headed right.

When I was just a kid, between the Great Depression and the Second War, things were a lot simpler. Just your name and the name of your town would get a letter to you; the mailman knew everybody. If you wanted to mail a letter and didn't have a stamp, you just left the letter and a few pennies in the mailbox. And the telephone numbers didn't strain your memory, either.

Our party line number was 24, and our phone ring one short, one long. There were seventeen families on our line, and we all had a different ring—one short, two longs; two shorts, two longs; like that. We could call each other just by picking up the receiver and, if nobody else was on the line, cranking the handle the right number of rings.

If we wanted to call somebody on another line, or long distance, then we rang one short. That was Central—Elsie Thayer. She was the operator, and had the switchboard in her kitchen. You just told her who you wanted, and she'd get 'em on the line. If there was trouble anywhere in the neighborhood, everybody'd hear one long, continuous ring. That meant a fire or accident, and that somebody needed help. You'd pick up the receiver to find out who and where.

To me, one of the worst things that's happened to America in the past fifty years is the private telephone line. The sense of community that we shared as a result of that party line is gone now. Of course it wasn't always convenient. It was kind of like a big family with one bathroom: you had to learn to accommodate one another. And of course we all knew each other's business. My lord, yes! Whenever the phone rang, no matter whose ring it was, almost everybody'd pick up. You could hear babies crying, clocks chiming, maybe a radio in the background. And the more people there were on the line, the louder you had to holler to make yourself heard. Once in a while one or another of the parties'd get just a little hot under the collar.

There was none of this soap opera stuff on the telephone in those days. The phone was for convenience only; and anybody who got a reputation for heavy personal chitchat could be sure of what nowadays they call a 100% market share whenever their ring came over the line.

Well, there was a couple who lived way at the end of the line, where the passable road dead-ended just under Hubbard Notch. Chisum, their name was. They rented the old Hubbard place and farmed it, but Lord! that was an awful tough pitch, and they couldn't've been more than just scraping by. It was beyond the end of the power lines, and there was just a hand pump at the kitchen sink for water. They sold wool every year, and swapped garden truck and syrup for groceries. I wouldn't call 'em unfriendly by any means, but they kept pretty much to themselves. Just a pair of regular old-time Yankees toughing it out on pure grit and patience.

They raised three kids up there—a couple of boys and a girl—but none of 'em stayed on. The boys found work in St. Johnsbury, and the daughter married and settled in Lancaster. So the two old folks were alone up there. Their ring was three shorts and a long. The only way I knew that was by the directory card, because Lord knows I never heard it.

Around Christmastime the calls on our line always got more interesting. You knew who was coming home for the holidays, and who wasn't, and if anybody was having a party. And one Christmas it turned out that things weren't too good up at the Hubbard place.

I'd seen Doc Barton's car go by several times in a couple of weeks, so I knew that somebody above us on the dirt road was sick. It had to be at the Chisums'; everybody else up there was on the phone pretty regular. So my wife and I kind of kept track of the one-ring calls to Central (Doc was on another line), and we found out that the old man was down, and pretty bad.

Then one night there was a three-short, one-long
ring. It was the Chisums' daughter in Lancaster. You
could hardly hear her. But she was saying that she
and her family weren't going to be able to come up
over Christmas. You know the excuses; we've all
heard 'em, and we've all used 'em one time or another: too busy, too far to travel. "Oh, dear," the old lady
said, "your father'll be so sad. Ralph and Bert can't
make it, either, and I know how he'd like to see you
all again." I didn't like the sound of that "again."
God, it broke my heart to hear it.

So on the morning before Christmas, when I was
up in the field getting a tree, I cut another little one,
besides. My wife put up a few Mason jars of soup,
and a casserole, and an extra apple pie. The kids had
painted up some milkweed pods bright red and made
strings of popcorn. During the afternoon we threw
everything into the old Chevy and headed up the
road.

It was snowing, and there was fresh snow on the
ground, but there were several sets of tire tracks in
the road. They kept going even beyond Caswells',
which was the last place before the Chisums'. And
when we pulled into the dooryard, there was about
four or five cars there already. There were lamps in
the windows. Smoke was rolling out of the chimney,
and you could hear voices inside, and laughing.

Out back by the woodshed, you could hear the
thunk of a splitting maul and the rumble of firewood
being stacked on the back porch. Joe Caswell and his
boy were carrying things into the smokehouse and
hanging them up. And—I wouldn't've believed it!—
the three Sheehan boys were wheeling barn dressing

out to the manure pile. Those birds'd never even clean their own barn unless their old man threatened 'em with a pistol! And then all at once we heard Canadian sleigh bells, getting louder, and here come Theo Corriveau in his pung, with his wife and at least six of the kids, and a couple of hind quarters of ven'son. And all these years he'd been pretending he didn't understand English!

What a party that was! The women were doing as good inside as the men outside. The kids were trimming the tree. Old Man Chisum was parked in a rocker by the cookstove with a brand-new quilt tucked around him, sipping a cup of ginshang tea and smelling like a fresh mustard plaster. The missus was smiling and looking kind of bewildered, and helping the women to find what they needed to get the dinner on the table.

Even the pastor and his wife were there. When he said grace, he said it with a voice so clear you'd never have suspected him of listening in on a party line. We ate sitting around the table, sitting on the floor—standing by the open door, it was so warm in the room.

Afterwards some of the women wanted to sing, but of course there was no organ. "Ah!" says Corriveau, holding up his finger. "I be right back!" And out the door he goes. A minute later he popped back in with a squeezebox—a concertina, he called it, or some such thing. All you had to do was hum a little bit of the carol you wanted to sing, and that son of a gun could play it!

During the evening the sky cleared and the moon come out, and we all drove home in a parade by moonlight, with our headlights off, and all the kids hanging their faces out the windows looking for the little sleigh in the sky.

No, don't tell me how wonderful all these new gadgets are. I know I could pick up my phone and call London or Tokyo direct. And nobody could listen in, unless he had a court order. But how I miss being able to just give my old wall phone a nice, long crank, wait for about a dozen clicks, and then wish all my neighbors at once a Merry Christmas!

# Gabby Smith

GABBY SMITH WAS BORN TO HIS HUMBLE station: genetically disposed to be the low man on any totem pole he might occupy. On a scale of 1 to 10, his social status was a minus 5.

Not quite so low that anybody actually would try to put him out of his misery, but low enough that, if you gave him a ride to work, you made sure there was a third guy in the car so Gabby would be in the back seat. It was bad enough to have everybody see him riding with you. It would have been unthinkable to arrive there with him beside you up front. Somebody might give it out that he was your friend.

And yet it's always amazed me how a crew of men—even the roughest of men—will suffer an obnoxious presence. Sometimes they'll even defend him against an outside attack or a cruel practical joke, almost as if to say, look, the poor guy's in tough enough shape already. Let him alone!

It could be, I suppose, because the low man occupies the spot that otherwise would have to be filled by somebody else. Or it could be out of an appreciation of the grace of providence that has spared the rest of us. Or even an unwittingly biblical forbearance: of him to whom little has been given, little is required.

Gabby had been given very little indeed. One of sixteen children brought up in a roadside shack without electricity, plumbing, or hope, he had early weighed his meager gifts and sensed the fruitlessness of attempting to rise above his assigned status. He had quit school at the earliest allowable age and begun a series of temporary laboring and logging jobs. And in a small town, where reputations grow early and cling forever, he quickly got one, as a petty thief.

About five-five he was, and scrawny; I doubt if he weighed 130. His face was rubious—he'd obviously had a severe case of acne. His teeth were black and green, with gaps. Big red nose and ears. And a voice! It was a nasal tenor mixture of a tobacco auctioneer and the taunting crows in *Dumbo*. And it never stopped clacking. Hence Gabby.

Gum ball machines, you put in two cents, and a gum ball comes out. Human beings, you put in two cents, you never know what you're going to get. All of us on the crew made about the same money, and it wasn't much. But we all had rubber boots, wool pants, and choppers; Gabby wore old shoes with adhesive-taped galoshes, gabardine trousers, and cotton gloves.

We had lunches in our lunch pails, and damn glad to have 'em, too, when the thermometer stayed down near zero all day. Poor old Gabby would drag some fragments of food out of his dirty coat pocket—half a bag of chips, maybe, or a piece of sandwich scavenged from an abandoned plate at The Little Tavern. Some of the older guys had pretty fancy lunches, with a thermos of soup, pickles wrapped in wax paper, and even a little dessert. One or two of them would always say, "By god, why does that woman put me up so much lunch? Gabby! Here! Eat this half a sandwich, will you? I can't take it home, or I won't get none tomorrow."

Sometimes in the evening, when we climbed into our icy cars to start home, he'd come out of the warm tool room, where the time clock was, and start shivering uncontrollably. Then Ray and I would take him into the front seat between us, and let the floor vent in Ray's old Pontiac blow hot air up Gabby's pants legs all the way home. It made us feel righteous, but it was the end of our conversation. It was like talking across a bonfire, where the heat scatters the molecules of the sound waves. Warm, and with a captive audience, Gabby was even more voluble than ever.

Still, he was a petty thief, and in our imaginations perpetually immersed in that aura. Automobile jacks, spare tires, tools, trash cans, axes, firewood, chain saw gas cans—they surrounded his shack and spilled out of his tumbledown shed. They were useless to him; he had duplicates of everything, and couldn't sell or fence anything in a town that small. Stealing was just something he did, to the virtual exclusion of every other activity—except occasionally working and always talking—and it was never mentioned between us.

The last time we worked together was the spring of 1959. I was already working in April, digging holes for new footings under an old summer hotel. Jud Whitney was the foreman. About mid-morning one day, Harvey Branch, the contractor, showed up in his truck with Gabby sitting beside him, pleased as punch, with a big, rotten-toothed smile.

"Jud," said Harvey. "I brought you another man."

"Good god, Harvey!" said Jud. "I don't want him! He'll steal every tool we give him!"

"Well, give him a wheelbarrow then," said Harvey. "He can't steal that! But he needs the work —got a family to feed—'y god, I want him on!"

At quitting time Gabby was still wheeling his wheelbarrow back and forth. But incredibly, there was one wheelbarrow missing. Jud drove back to the job shortly after dark and sat there in his truck till Gabby and his wife came in their old car to retrieve it from the woods.

I saw him one last time years later. Passing through town headed somewhere, I stopped for lunch at the diner at the foot of Spruce Hill. A few minutes later in came Gabby, holding one arm with his other hand. "Gimme a cup of black coffee!" he shouted at the counter girl. "Hi, Bill. How ya doin'?" He never did get my name right.

"Hi, Gab," I waved. "What's wrong with your arm?"

"Just wrecked m'car up on top the hill. Broke my goddam arm. Gotta get sobered up 'fore the troopers get here."

He'd run two miles down the hill, and now he was gulping coffee as fast as he could. But it didn't look as though he was going to make it.

"Anybody else in the wreck?" the waitress asked him.

"Yeah, my wife and kid. I think they're okay, though. They were movin' when I left."

*Pax vobiscum,* Gabby.

# RIP, Big Jim

*Deliverance* OCCUPIES A SPACE ON MY AUTO-graphed-book shelf, in the Fiction and Poetry De-partment. Its author died the other day. So I took it out this evening and read again the scribbled inscrip-tion on the title page.

"To Will Lang—" it says (the "W" written with three swoops instead of two, like pointy waves in a child's picture of water), "at the beginning—James Dickey."

I haven't the foggiest notion what he meant by that. It may have been something he wrote routinely, without the foggiest notion himself what he meant by it. I flattered myself for a while that the poet, rec-ognizing in me a kindred sensitivity, had entrusted me with an obscure profundity that only he and I shared. But I got over that long ago, and gave up wondering.

James Dickey blared briefly though my life some twenty-odd years ago—like a Jeep going by with the stereo turned up full blast—and made me aware as almost never before of how much a Yankee I am—or at least how little a Southerner I am.

A phone call started it—a call from a dear friend, a Dartmouth professor, a poet himself, and an exceed-ingly gentle and spiritual man whose poetry floats above the earth as delicately, colorfully as the aurora. About a month earlier he'd been seriously trauma-tized by three days with a wild egomaniac of a visit-ing poet—Ted Hughes, I think it was—that had left him almost prostrate for days afterward. Now he'd been assigned to entertain another overpowering personality.

"Can you help me out with this?" he almost plead-ed. "Mr. Dickey has brought his twelve-string guitar with him, and he says that tomorrow morning he'd like to play with somebody local who knows some of the old folk songs."

Mr. Dickey had not yet risen when I got there after breakfast. But around nine we heard somebody upstairs knock over a few empty beer bottles onto the hardwood bedroom floor. Shortly afterward he descended, rumpled, huge, and ill, with his twelve-string guitar on his arm. He looked like a cowboy who didn't yet remember losing his horse in a poker game the night before.

We played and sang most of the morning, with the sun streaming in the French windows—"Pore Little Ellen," "Rosewood Casket," "Naomi Wise." He leaned less toward unrequited love and useless sentiment than to unfortunate maidens and their violent ends. And, working his way through a six-pack of Bud, he leaned more and more toward the horizontal as noon approached.

We lunched at the Inn with a few students and a normally distinguished English professor with a Southern accent that deepened appreciably as the visiting fireman told one chicken-pluckin' story after another. Old, dirty, corny stories; surely they'd heard them before. But they all laughed like madmen and practically fell out of their chairs after each punch line. The professor carried on the worst. It was like watching a grizzly bear play with a ground squirrel— the same grizzly that, when it got serious, could describe the horror of forced sodomy, and death by a broadhead arrow, with such detail that you wonder he could have done it without having seen it. But I knew that he had seen it, on the screen of his mind; and I had often wondered how any corporal body could endure living with such a mind. Not only that; he had to know they were kissing his ass because he was famous, and not because his jokes were funny. How could anyone live with that?

After lunch we drove around the Connecticut Valley in my little Volkswagen Squareback, and he waxed autobiographical—not entirely truthfully, as it turned out later. He'd played football at Clemson and Vanderbilt. At the tag end of World War II, he told me, he'd flown a P-61 Black Widow night fighter on bombing missions over the Japanese mainland. "I'd drop my incendiaries on little bamboo Japanese villages," he said, "and then I was supposed to fly back over and verify the damage. And everything was on fire. Houses, trees, people—women and children— running around on fire." That was probably more than a twenty-two-year-old should have been asked to do, which I think is what he was trying to say. And it would have helped immensely, if it had been true, to explain the threatening turmoil of his poetry and his novel. But he hadn't been a pilot. It didn't matter. His fiction was as revealing as the truth in explaining the source of all that tension.

In the afternoon he was insistent that we drive to the middle school and park where we could see the children coming out. "My god!" he cried, "aren't they beautiful! And look! Almost every one of those little girls is blond-haired and blue-eyed!" He was right. I had never noticed that before. It was like his poetry: the fetid lust and hate of the cretinous characters lurking inside southern barns were creatures of our own imaginations who would never see the light of our northern days. He had a way of scraping scales from our eyes. And the vision was disturbing.

That evening there was a little soiree for him at the shy professor's house. I wondered how Dickey could endure being so imprecisely caressed. But he seemed to bask in it. A young English professor came in, his voice dripping with southern honey as he greeted the great man.

"Yo fum Sath Calanah!" exclaimed Dickey, and the two of them went into an incredible hand-slapping honkie version of an Amos-and-Andy routine: checking relatives and lineage, mutual friends at the Citadel, and names of hated publishers. Then, suddenly Dickey turned right around and cut the young professor dead. He wilted like a hibiscus.

Someone, desperately making conversation, asked my friend, the shy poet, how his new pet raccoon was doing. "Well," he answered, " he's still having a few problems, but he seems much better."

"What?" said Dickey. "You got a pet coon? Goddam! Bring that little scuttah in heah!"

The baby raccoon was dutifully produced and placed in his lap. It was restless—it had been ill—and after a few moments of petting, scuttled up the sleeve of Dickey's blazer, across the back of his neck, and down the other arm, shitting virtually every inch of the way. The restlessness had been the result of diarrhea; the coon left a a perfect U-shaped trail of excrement as it went.

"Goddam! cried the Southern poet again. He couldn't decide whether to do something or just sit perfectly still till help arrived. The other poet dashed with me toward the kitchen, raccoon in hand, to grab some paper towels. He handed me the coon and began yanking a long strip of towels off the roller. He was beaming. "Can't fool a dumb animal, can you?" he murmured.

Rest in peace at last, Jim. I mean it. You taught me more than you'll ever know.

# Children of the Air

It takes less than a day to travel from northern New England to Texas. The shock of breakfasting in Etna, New Hampshire, and having supper in Dallas is intense. Still, I spent part of my youth working in Texas, and thus part of my heart still lies here.

Dallas is a brawny, self-important city, ringed and pierced by arterial highways that give it the air of one of the fanciful, futuristic cities we used to see in *Buck Rogers*. I leave it behind me as fast as I can, my feet and imagination already headed westward as soon as I collect my luggage. The very largest General Motors suburban vehicle seems to be the State Car; and the compact that I normally rent feels tiny, insignificant, and unsafe. Several lanes of traffic stream past a backdrop of car dealerships, steak houses, and oil field equipment suppliers at better than seventy miles an hour. A large banner snaps at the head of a very high flagpole. As we come abreast, I chance a glance at its legend: JESUS. Below it, a huge sign: MULTIPLEX CHAPEL, REV. JIM GORMAN.

This trip was a pilgrimage for me. My wife had come along, as much, I think, to see what it is about the place that so moves me as just to keep me company. We spent the night about an hour west of Dallas, and in the morning headed west again. Old familiar names began to flow past—Dublin, Comanche, Blanket, Early. A little before noon we stopped on the edge of Brownwood, picked up take-out barbecue for four, and headed north into the fringes of the west Texas hill country. The plains fell away to our right, and on our left, dry, cobbly slopes of iron-stained Breckenridge limestone shouldered up to the road. The shape of the land stirred in me a faint recognition and old, vague memories. We were almost there.

This was the country I came to over fifty years ago, like Jacob traveling to Mesopotamia 2700 years ago, to work for a rancher to win a wife. Jacob worked fourteen years and came home with two wives, a concubine, a million sheep, and enough kids to beget the twelve tribes of Israel. I came home with a broken-down pickup truck, a headful of lovely memories, and a lifelong friend—the rancher.

Bransford is almost 98 now, stooped and frail, and freshly missing an eye to cancer. His wife, Mary Eloise, had added a note to one of his last letters. It was time to go see him again.

In the middle of nowhere, along a buzzard-haunted county highway, a dirt lane led off to the east. I wasn't sure it was the right one, but my hands turned the wheel. Past the cattle guard, huge half-Brahma cows grazed with their calves in the shade of live oak trees. Half a mile farther on, beside a pond, stood the little house.

Phoebes were nesting in the front porch, hummingbirds vibrated over beds of bluebonnet and Indian blanket in the dooryard, and little striped lizards darted through the sand at the entrance to the truck shed. We sat in the dining room, with the gas heater on to ease the old man's chill.

While Mary Eloise and Mother slipped into the parlor for a Bible study, he talked of old times—as a young cowboy on a cattle boat to Asia; years of penury at Princeton Seminary; the long-ago discovery of oil under his father's land that has sustained him modestly ever since; the exciting years as a missionary in China. He spoke of the layer of ancient volcanic ash he's found at the top of the Permian, and of the geological formation that's been named for him. We dined on barbecue, washed down with iced tea, and finished with a Dr. Pepper float.

After lunch, he tipped his head toward me and declared in the sage and confidential tone I remembered so well, "Will, a man with one eye is more than half blind. Especially when he's got a nose like mine blocking out more'n half the view.

"But you know, I sometimes see things out of the corner of the eye that isn't there. And the other day, on the way to Cross Plains, I saw the doggonedest thing. I happened to glance to my right, and—I swear—there was a little boy running along beside my pickup. Next time I looked, there were three or four children there.

"They were smiling and waving at me, just as pleasant, y'know. And when I speeded up, they just lifted up off the ground and kept right up; and after a while, there was another little boy beside the left-hand door.

"When I got to sister Lydia's, they were all around me in the dooryard, laughing and talking. And while I was having a cup of tea with Lydia, sitting at the table, there was the sweetest little girl—two years old, maybe—standing right beside me and looking up at me."

His good eye glistened. "Eloise tells me I shouldn't go on about this. Folks'll know I'm beginning to slip. But, shoot, Will, I'm going to enjoy old age just as much as I can." He smiled thinly at the fear crouching in the corner of the kitchen.

Just before we left, Mary Eloise took Mother aside and said, "He doesn't know it; but I know where those children came from.

"The other morning we were watching the news on the television, and the pictures came on of the bombed-out building in Oklahoma City. The announcer told about all the children in the day care center that were buried in the rubble. And Bransford just sat there, and cried and cried . . ."

We drove back down the lane through the Brahma cattle and past hundreds of my memories. Crossing the branch, I fancied I could see children playing in the opaque green water. They were weeping. And so was I.

# Randallsville

I hear the accuser roar the ills that I have done.
I know them well and a thousand more;
    Jehovah findeth none.
He findeth none, He findeth none.
I've been washed in the blood of His Son.

THE LATE WINTER SUN SHONE THROUGH a heavy snow squall and flooded the crowded frame church building with light the color of cream. Up front, facing the congregation, an upright piano and an electronic keyboard flanked four guitars and a tambourine. An overhead transparency projector cast the words of the old hymn onto the lime-green wall behind them.

The singing congregation stood in family groups, some parents holding infants; others, eyes closed, their kids stiff in Sunday clothes at their sides, raising their hands in ecstasy.

Outside, the wind made the most of the fresh snow, swirling it across the wide fields and leaving it in sharp little drifts across the roads, deeper up against the windward banks and tapering to wet tips toward the far side. Crows stalked along the rows of stubble and probed with their beaks. Their feathers ruffled when they turned tail to the wind.

Randallsville sits in a flat-bottomed valley open to

the north and south. During the last glacial age, the terminus of the ice sheet was in equilibrium near here for many years; which is to say that it melted backward under the attack of the warming climate at much the same rate it advanced under the impulse of the great ice-making machinery far to the north. The effect was like that of a hay elevator with nobody at the top end to take away the bales. The boulders, sand, and gravel that it bore were dumped here in almost incomprehensible amounts, in some places thousands of feet thick.

The landscape is a skeleton of ancient limestone fleshed out with gravel and clay. Small streams choked with alder thickets ripple over gravel beds in U-shaped valleys. Where great chunks of glacial ice broke off and were buried in drift, their slow melting formed little kettle hole lakes that still swarm with ducks and geese in season. What a racket there must have been here in the springtimes 10,000 years ago! —when this was the edge of the ice, and dark, fur-clad human beings, following the herds of their now-extinct prey, were still only a whispered, ominous presence in the land.

It's quiet here now, with a slight ache to it, like the quiet mustiness of an abandoned house. The only sounds are those of a distant truck engine, the calling of crows, and the wind in bare maple branches. The hardwood forests on the steep hillsides, the fields and pastures in the valleys, lie waiting for spring. Here and there a barn and silo punctuate the brown-stained whiteness. Some of the silos are steel, new and blue and emblazoned with the names of their makers and owners: HARVESTORE—*Dick and Dody*

*Doxtater.* Others are of gray, weathered wood, banded in rusting steel hoops and leaning crazily away from the prevailing wind.

A couple of miles north, all the brooks run northward and reach the sea at the Gulf of St. Lawrence. Here, the infant Chenango River begins its long journey to the Susquehanna and eventually Chesapeake Bay. There is no hint of either of those destinies in the alder clots and stubble fields of Madison County. The houses are nineteenth-century stone, Greek Revival or Victorian; many of the stores and gas stations are straight from the 1930s; and the orange tractors hooked to manure spreaders and the white cement milkhouses beside the roads seem eternal.

The preacher opened the Bible on the lectern and read the text, from Malachi: " . . . the Lord has borne witness against you on behalf of the wife of your youth . . . Keep watch on your spirit, and do not be unfaithful to the wife of your youth." It was going to be a sermon on marriage. I felt a brief, but profound surge of relief that, in spite of everything and after all these years, I was sitting next to the wife of my youth. Knowing this to be a church that rarely, if ever, preaches from one text, but instead bolsters it with many others, I wondered if, in this wintry season, he'd get to my favorite text on the subject.

Sure enough, in a few minutes he did: "Ecclesiastes 4:9—'Two are better than one . . . for if they fall, the one will lift up his fellow: but woe to him that is alone when he falleth . . . [and] if two lie together, then they have heat: but how can one be warm alone?'" I nudged the wife of my youth; she trod hard on my toe.

In many ways the second half of this century has passed by this valley. A few miles west, Sunday-morning Syracuse and its burgeoning satellites bulge and bustle with bypasses and beltways and suburban malls and urban blight. Five minutes to the east, the Colgate Inn serves a genteel Sunday brunch to students and their visiting parents. To the north, the New York Thruway carries away the commerce and modernization that once rumbled through these glacial hills. Here, the only hints that time has not stood still are the new automobiles outside the church, an occasional satellite video dish, and the skeletons of dead elms along the fence rows.

Inside the church, it might have been a hundred years ago. They prayed for farmers; for a sister injured in an accident; for the sick; for the newly converted and the unsaved loved ones; for a job for Jim. As an outsider—and an Episcopalian, at that—I get nervous about unanimity. But the sense of personal and communal strength and vigor pervading the place was one that I have not felt in very many places for a long time: the idea of each person being an essential building block, supporting and supported, in a structure far greater than each—greater, even, than all together.

The squall passed. A patch of blue spread across the sky, big enough, at last, to make a pair of Dutchman's breeches. The musicians stood up again. The overhead projector flicked on.

Because He lives, I can face tomorrow . . .

# *Uh-Oh!*

I SHOULD HAVE KNOWN BETTER. NOW, after twenty more years as a contractor, I do. But the voice on the phone was throaty and seductive—like Greta Garbo with an eastern European accent.

"Ve are renting gows in Hanower. Toilet in bathroom iss loose, viggles. Landlord not awailable. You can come feex, yes?"

Can you hear the alarm bells in those simple sentences, the subtle traps for the unwary and inexperienced? Here are three of them: First, it's rarer than a blue moon for a toilet to be only "loose, viggles." Second, the bill for the work will be sent to the landlord, who is "not awailable." And third, only an idiot would say, "Sure, I can fix it!" without first looking at the problem.

"Sure, I can fix it!" I said. Within an hour I was gazing at a floor so rotten that even the joists beneath it were gone. The toilet was teetering precariously, supported only by the four-inch copper line rising from the cellar. Turned out that Ms. Garbo's husband, in a rush to catch a plane to Chicago, had discovered the problem the hard way that very morning.

"Wow!" I thought. "Won't the landlord be happy that I have found and corrected this potentially lethal problem!"

It is best I draw a veil of discretion over the ensuing technical, social, and financial agonies of that situation. It was an eye-opener in many ways. I have tried hard ever since not to blink, and have eliminated the word "Sure!" from my vocabulary, except in irony.

Because I've found over the years that there are very few little problems in malfunctioning buildings. There are only little symptoms: a tiny pyramidal pile of sawdust under a hole in a support timber (carpenter ants); an outside door that drags the floor when it swings in (rotten sill); "spongy" tile on a shower wall; icicles hanging down inside the eaves.

I once had a dentist, years ago, whose favorite expression, as he moved from tooth to tooth with his probe, was "Uh-oh." I resolved then, as the clownish fool drove me into depression, never to use that expression myself within hearing of the owner of the premises I was inspecting.

"Mm-hm" and "Eyah" are two good and noncommittal alternatives, with a tremendous number of possible variations in inflection. "Oh, wow!" is not so hot. "Well, well, well . . . " sounds fairly intelligent. "Holy Toledo!" does not.

The area of the house where these are most often spoken—that creates far and away the greatest number of problems and expense per cubic inch—is the aforementioned bathroom. It's an innocent-looking little space that, once fiddled with, turns out to be a slippery slope to ruin. Messing with it is like picking a fight with the littlest guy in a barroom, and then discovering that he's the lightweight champion of the world.

A typical scenario: Ms. B calls to tell me that she's gotten a real deal on a vinyl flooring remnant for the master bath, and needs the toilet and baseboards temporarily removed so that the vinyl can be installed over the existing flooring. I enter the room to do the job, and discover that the fixtures are avocado-colored. I should leave right then, but don't.

The baseboards have been glued to the wall, and when removed, tear the sheetrock paper, which must now be patched. And when I pull the toilet, I discover its base is cracked and has been leaking. So now we're up to a new toilet and new plywood underlayment.

New avocado-colored fixtures have, for a very good reason, disappeared from the face of the earth. After consultation, Ms. B decides to change to white. This makes the other fixtures look strange. So now we're up to a new lavatory and tub, as well.

The tub can't be removed without taking off the wall tile first. And the wall behind the tile is too far gone and rough to reuse. So now we're up to deciding whether to retile or install a fiberglass tub and shower unit.

We remove the lavatory from the existing vanity, and I hear Ms. B say, "What do you suppose a new vanity would cost? I've never liked that one, anyway." I direct her to a supplier, and she returns with a new vanity and medicine cabinet. The old medicine cabinet has a built-in light; the new one doesn't. Off she goes for a new light fixture, while I call the electrician.

She comes back with a light fixture and a ceiling exhaust fan, besides. The electrician takes one look at the wiring in the existing cabinet. "Uh-oh," he says. (He should be a dentist, but he'd make less money.) "Two-wire," he announces. " No ground. Gotta run back to the panel."

Which turns out to be overloaded already. "Can't touch this," he announces (and he's not kidding; legally he can't). "And it won't handle a sub-panel. Have to put in a new entrance. Be a good opportunity to bury those service wires."

In the corner of the dining room stands the roll of vinyl flooring on which Ms. B got such a great deal. Out by the curb, a power company truck is at work on the pole; a backhoe and dump truck are tearing up and carrying away the yard; and the carpenter's and electrician's vans stand with doors agape in the driveway. The sheetrocker will be here Monday, the tile man (who never comes when he says he's going to) says he'll be here on Wednesday. Mr. B, who thought new vinyl in the bathroom was a good idea, will be home from Boston Thursday.

The plumber arrives, clipboard in hand, to make a list of the parts he needs. He kneels down, smashes a hole through the sheetrock of the wall behind the shower and tub controls, and gazes in at the plumbing and valves. "Uh-oh," he says.

# Qurluktuk

*Qurluktuk is the name in Inuktitut of a village at the mouth of the Coppermine River on the north coast of Canada. It means "where water falls down," a reference to a tremendous rapid about twelve kilometers upstream. The village's name is spelled "Kugluktuk" on the local school and post office, thanks to a tin-eared bureaucrat in Ottawa. Pronounced this way, it means "where two people jump up when you goose them." So whenever you hear a native say it, you'll see an ironic little grin at the corner of his mouth; no European can grin as ironically as a native American.*

*The great rapid is called Bloody Falls. It was named that by the explorer Samuel Hearne in 1771 after his Chipewyan guides surprised a group of Inuit fishing there and slaughtered as many as they could catch. Pain and misunderstanding have a long history here.*

MARK AYALIK IS TEN YEARS OLD. He stands shyly in the front doorway of his house and, as I approach, leans on his mother and runs one arm around her hips as if he were about to dodge behind her. His face is dark as a black walnut rifle stock, his eyes ripe olives, his teeth a startling white. With a fur hat on, he could be Mongolian. He smiles the customary U-shaped Inuit smile and edges slightly out of sight.

How odd we must seem, we four bearded old men from another world where there are trees, automobiles, and all the wonderful things he has seen for years on the television set in his living room. Our faces are more exotic to him than his to us —*Qallunait*, his ancestors called us when they first met us: "Dog-faces." His ancestors trekked eastward from Asia several thousand years ago, following the good hunting at the end of the last Ice Age, and spread in only a few generations all the way across the American Arctic. Our ancestors sailed westward in open boats only one thousand years ago. They met during a rare climatic optimum at the height of the Viking Age; and then, when the cold returned, shrank back from each other for another 700 years.

Mark and I look at one another just as those ancestors must have then: as through a pane of glass. From his point of view, I might as well be from the moon; and of his life in Qurluktuk I know virtually nothing. There is a double difference between us: national and ethnic. I very much want him to like me, as most elderly men hope children will like them. And he, sensing that we are paying guests in his house, no doubt also senses his mother's nervous need to please us.

The eastern end of Qurluktuk rises to a basalt bluff above the mouth of the Coppermine River. Standing there and gazing across the wide, shallow estuary, you can see on the sandy flat beyond the opposite bank what look like regular rows of cabins, or a mobile home park. When you finally realize what they are, you also realize that—like everything in this land without trees—they're much closer than they seem. They're the crosses and mounds in the village graveyard.

They're arranged in two groups, quite separate from each other. One group, composed of only simple pole crosses, is the resting place of the village's Roman Catholics; the other, with more ornate crosses of lumber, brass nameplates, and piles of flowers on the mounds, is for Anglicans. Even in death the people of this tiny hamlet are divided by outsiders; and I can't see them so without feeling a deep frustration and embarrassment.

The day we got here, the ocean was too rough outside the bar to head east in the little schooner moored in the river mouth; so our host Larry, Mark, and Mark's mother, Helen, climbed into a small aluminum outboard to visit the cemetery. I asked if I might come along.

No one, in this land of permafrost, is buried deeply. Here and there, as here in Qurluktuk, will occur a sandy or silty delta, where a shallow grave may be scooped out a few feet down. But then suddenly the shovels scrape against frozen ground, and that's the end of it. Out on the tundra, we occasionally encounter traditional burials: a skeleton faintly visible inside a mound of rocks, with a few desiccated or rotting belongings arranged nearby—a kayak frame, rifle, spear, or soapstone lamp. This ancient custom of decorating the graves with the deceased's possessions has carried over to this village. An old and rusted .22 caliber rolling-block rifle lies in the sand beside one mound. A surprising number of mounds are covered with dolls and tiny metal race cars.

It seems somehow appropriate, here where nothing but summer disappears quickly, to be constantly surrounded by reminders of mortality. Often we spot injured caribou, unable to travel, and doomed. On the routes of the annual caribou migrations, the ground is virtually covered with broken bones for dozens of square miles; and now and then we come upon the massive skull of a musk ox.

Larry, Helen, Mark, and I landed on the far side of the river, tied the boat's painter to a willow bush, and clambered up the sandy bluff. The graveyards are set fairly back from the eroding bank, with a view of the village to the west and Coronation Gulf to the north. We tramped through knee-high willows and birches to the far side of the Anglican cemetery. Here Helen stopped at three fresh graves, mounded high with plastic flowers and children's toys. She stood gazing at them for a few minutes, her head shaking slightly from side to side; then knelt beside each one in turn, straightening the wind-tossed toys and seeming to pray, while Larry knelt with one arm around her. Mark, who is rarely still for a moment, picked up clods of silty clay, tossed them into the air, and batted at them with a piece of lath. Whenever he hit one, it disappeared in a little puff of beige dust against the sun.

Qurluktuk was for centuries a gathering place of the Inuit during the annual char run. Samuel Hearne was the first European to see it, the day after the massacre at Bloody Fall. He did not find the copper he was seeking for the Hudson's Bay Company, and walked home again to Hudson Bay. John Franklin, the ill-starred British naval officer who left his bones somewhere east of here on his last expedition, passed through in 1821 in an early attempt to chart a north-west passage. Just after the turn of this century, a Canadian expedition under Vilhjalmur Stefansson "discovered" these people and named them Copper Inuit, after the deposits of native copper still supposed to be lying about on the ground. Roman Catholic missionaries followed, and even though two of them were murdered in 1913, the church persisted. The Hudson's Bay Company arrived in 1927, the Royal Canadian Mounted Police in 1932.

The *qallunait* brought civilization: a cash economy, grocery stores, alcohol, and competing versions of Christianity. Qurluktuk now has a video rental store and as many two-cycle engines per capita as any town on earth. In the Anglican church, a Caucasian Jesus in bare feet stands in the snow above the altar beckoning to fur-clad Inuit with dog teams. The Prayer Book includes a petition for the health of the Queen and her family. Alcoholism, wife-beating, and child abuse are epidemic.

Mark slowly became accustomed to us. We rode together on Larry's schooner for several days, looking for char at the mouths of rivers. He played with Leggos down in the forward cabin, swung from the cargo boom—he's going to be a powerful, athletic man—and slept under a robe out on deck. He's a demon fisherman, with a two-handed spin-casting delivery and sanguine expectation of success. When he saw us catching char with our fly rods, he began flailing his spinning rod back and forth in imitation; it wasn't safe to get anywhere near him. I asked him for the present of his name written on a little piece of paper. It took him ten painful minutes to write it. I told him I would cherish it, and I do.

On March 26, four months before we met Mark, his father (Helen's ex-husband) went mad during a drinking binge and shot to death three of Mark's brothers and sisters. Those were the three graves, decorated with fading toys, that we had visited. He pointed the rifle into Mark's face and shouted, "Get out!" Mark got out, and his father shot himself to death.

*There's no way of knowing, watching Mark swing from the cargo boom, how much he remembers of that, or what it means to him; whether it troubles his dreams in the fading light of late summer, here on the north shore of the civilized world.*

# Pastor Youngblood

A NEW PREACHER COMING TO OUR LITTLE church here in the middle of nowhere always reminds me of a car driving fast down a narrow road in late September. The wind of its passing sets the dry leaves to whirling every which way. Then after a while they settle down again pretty much where they were before. 'Course, you've got to consider, this is Vermont, so there isn't quite as great a stir here as there is in some places. Here, it's as if maybe the leaves are just a little wet when the car comes by.

Our new pastor's been here about a year now. Started the Sunday after Labor Day. Fresh out of seminary he was, and greener'n grass. Name of Youngblood. Good name for him.

Well, this Youngblood hit town with more ideas than a puppy in a chicken yard. And I must say he was a likable kid. Preached a pretty good sermon, too, his first Sunday, on the conversion of Saint Paul. Even kept old Manning Moody awake.

I suppose we should have been tipped off by his car. It was a little tan-colored diesel Rabbit with bumper stickers front and back. "BAN THE BOMB!" was the biggest one. Then two more: "NO NUKES" and "GET THE CIA OUT OF NICARAGUA." You don't see too much of that on the cars of folks who've always lived here. We get more excited about bovine growth hormone and school taxes and the cost of electricity.

Well, we had our first meeting of the board of elders a couple of weeks after Youngblood got here. He announced he was going to reorganize the church into a bunch of commissions, just the way Christ had (Youngblood was right too; I looked it up). Each elder was to be in charge of a different commission. I'd kept the church books ever since 1947, and that wouldn't change. Except that now I was to be the Treasurer and Chairman of the Finance Commission.

Elmer Hoskins, who hardly ever misses a Sunday, always keeps a plumber's helper behind the seat of his truck because the men's toilet seems to get stopped up almost every Sunday. Well, now Elmer was appointed Chairman of the Property Commission. And so on, all down the line, till the pastor got to Vern Sutton.

Vern's kind of a quiet fellow, don't say much. Farmer, about 60 years old. Very handsome man, red-faced from being outdoors most of the time. My wife says he looks a lot like Gary Cooper, but I don't know about that. Husky, with a big Adam's apple and great thick forearms. Walks with a heavy limp. Doesn't have any particular leanings or talent to speak of. So Pastor Youngblood announced he was now the Chairman of the Social Action Commission.

"I want to hold some seminars this fall," he explained. "Encounter groups, where we can share our thoughts and feelings and speak frankly with each other. We'll spend whole weekends discussing and acting out issues of concern to the Christian Church

—world hunger, sanctuary for Central American refugees, world peace. A church that isn't involved in addressing these issues in this day and age is hiding its head in the sand. The Church has to take public stands as part of its Christian witness to the world." You can imagine how much excitement that caused. Although, to be honest, I haven't seen that bunch ever get excited about anything—except, maybe, when we got the estimate for rewiring the church, and the next week we found out that old Effie Fairbanks'd left us $75,000 in her will.

A few days later, on a Sunday afternoon, Youngblood asked me for directions to Vern's place. He was going to pay a pastoral visit. It was too complicated to describe; he'd never've got there. So I took him out myself. 'Twas at the end of a dirt road way up on a side hill.

We pulled up into the yard, and old three-legged Barney, Vern's dog, come hopping out to meet us, his tail banging away like a carpet beater.

"Well!" said the preacher, bending down to pet him. "What happened to you, old guy?"

"He was a stray, I guess. Vern found him starving in a coyote trap couple of winters ago. Leg was frozen. Vet wanted to put him down. Vern said no, he'd keep him."

Vern's wife, Mary, met us on the porch. Now, she's without a doubt the nicest person you'd ever want to meet anywhere, but there's this about her: She's also probably the plainest woman you've ever seen. I could see Youngblood looking at her and wondering. She took us out to the kitchen and perked coffee while Vern came in and washed up.

A big one-eyed tiger cat jumped up in Young-blood's lap while we talked, laid down, and began to purr as loud as a lawn mower. He couldn't help but pet her. Then I saw him cutting his eyes at a man in a chair by the window reading a comic book, his lips moving silently. The man looked up and smiled and nodded when we come in, but he hadn't said any-thing, and then he went right back to his comic book. And I noticed Youngblood's gaze dart every so often to the gold medal in the dime store frame sit-ting on the mantel.

Vern and Mary were as pleasant as pie, but I could see the pastor wasn't getting anywhere with his weekend seminars. He wanted all the participants to come down to the church hall Friday evenings, and then camp out there till Sunday after church: sleep-ing on the floor, cooking in the church kitchen, sit-ting in a circle on folding chairs during the discus-sions. I was thinking as he talked, I sure hope Elmer Hoskins'll come with his plunger!

Problem was, of course, that Youngblood had no idea what farmers do. Vern and Mary, for example— there wasn't any way they could leave their cows for the weekend. And during spring planting, haying, and harvest they couldn't leave for even a few min-utes. And it wasn't just them. Elmer couldn't leave the hardware store on Saturday; that was his busiest day of the week. Nobody, really, except maybe a cou-ple of the elderly ladies and one retired couple from away, could take that much time off from their work. Making a living here, I'll tell you: it ain't just dancing around a maypole. So they finally got it whittled down to a few Sunday afternoons, and they ended up scheduling a meeting in October to discuss whether the church should break the law by offering sanctuary to Nicaraguan refugees. Youngblood and I left about half-past four and headed for home.

"What a . . . a . . . fascinating couple!" he started. "How long have they been married?" I knew what he was thinking: not exactly a matched set.

"Oh, only about three years. Vern's first wife, Sara, died of a brain tumor. God! it was an awful thing, poor woman! Mary was a friend of theirs, never'd been married, or even asked, I guess. But Vern married her, about six months after Sara died, and it's worked out pretty good for both of 'em.

"You probably want to ask me about the man with the comic book. That's Freddie Dance. He was a foundling up at the county home . . . oh, probably forty years ago now. Nobody'd take him because he was retarded, you know. So Vern and Sara took him, and he's been there ever since. Good hired man, steadiest there ever was, and you can see he's happy there. He'll be joining the choir at Christmas time; he loves to sing Christmas carols. Vern's provided for him for afterwards, too."

"And what was that medal in the frame up on the mantel?" asked Youngblood.

"Oh, that's Vern's Congressional Medal of Honor. He was a conscientious objector in the Korean War, so they made him a medic. I guess there was a night attack, and he went out under fire to rescue a whole squad that'd been shot up. You've seen his limp? He was wounded right away, but he brought 'em all back to their lines, one at a time, before he collapsed himself."

Youngblood sat still and looked out the window while my old Buick rumbled back down the mountain. I didn't say nothing, either. Here in Vermont we don't believe in talking unless we can improve on the silence.

# Dad's Junk

We're headed home through Vermont, my wife and I, eastward over Mendon Gap between Rutland and Woodstock. The fresh snow isn't deep at all, but it's blowing hard and slippery as grease in the warm temperatures. Every few miles we spot flashing lights up ahead and pass a car or truck off the road in an awkward posture. At our slow speed, we're unlikely to get home before the post office closes. Whether we do or not, it'll be awfully nice just to get there.

It's not a long drive from our house in New Hampshire to Syracuse, New York. Six hours, more or less, and a good bit of that on four-lane highways. But the route passes through the ever-busier centers of Rutland, Lake George, and Amsterdam; and to someone attuned, as I am, to the leisurely meters of Etna, it's a tremendous hassle, especially during weekends, holidays, bad weather, and peak tourist seasons.

But it was my old man's 89th birthday yesterday, and we don't see him enough, anyway. Normally I'd wait for a birthday divisible by five before tackling a weekday trip. The other day, though, my sister's voice on the answering machine told me that he'd had another fainting spell. So we moved some appointments around, packed the van, and hit the road.

He'd passed out in church this time, she said, right in the middle of the sermon. (This had particular significance for him, because he was giving the sermon. I couldn't help but reflect that nobody had slept through that one; but probably nobody could recall what it had been about, either.) He'd hit his head and strained his back when he fell, but only the back was bothering him. Plus the fact that the doctors said there wasn't much they could do about the fainting.

At my time of life, as I look around to find that most of my friends have lost their parents, I consider it a blessing that I still have one. It's good genetic news. On top of that, he's always been a robust, athletic kind of guy—old photographs of his youth show him wearing high leather boots with a jack-knife pocket on one; playing football; climbing cliffs; and shoveling wheat—and I'd hoped, I suppose, that it would never end; that, in fact, he might even survive me.

He's been deaf since the age of ten, the result of spinal meningitis in the days before antibiotics. My mother was deaf, too, from the same cause, so my sister and I grew up speaking sign language. It didn't seem at all out of the ordinary to us until we got old enough for the rest of the world to assure us that it was. He graduated from Gallaudet College, and tried working for a while in his father's pharmacy, and after that at a meat packing plant. Then an elderly priest, a missionary to deaf congregations, persuaded him to study for the Episcopal ministry.

That was the start of fifty years on the road, driving from town to town all over New York State, with as many as five services on a Sunday. He was a great driver, proud of the fact that the deaf had better accident records than hearing drivers. It was a big deal to him how many times he'd driven the equivalent of around the world and to the moon. Now he's retired, but still fills in wherever there's a hole. And I suppose that's what got him this time: standing up to preach and lifting his arms to sign, there just wasn't enough blood going to his brain.

When digital watches came in, with their stopwatch mode, he used to time himself for the run from the kitchen, out through the garage to the curb with the rubbish, and back. That ended the day he gave the garage door too big a heave. He couldn't hear it rumble, of course; and when it came back down, it knocked him cold. So his last run was a did-not-finish.

He hasn't had any natural balance since his inner ear was disconnected from his brain. So he's always relied on a visual horizon for equilibrium. But now, with his eyes less acute and his legs less nimble, he has to shuffle his feet to feel the floor beneath him. I remember how I used to have to double-time to keep up with him, and feel a keen pang of regret.

When my wife and I got to his home in mid-afternoon, I had brooded so long about his condition that I was astonished by the vigor of his embrace. Clearly, though much is taken, much abides. We talked, and I was careful to sit with the light behind him and in my face, so he could see me better when I signed. I avoided concept discussions, complicated arguments, and people and places he didn't know; they require spelling words like "transubstantiation" and "Millinocket," and he doesn't see all the letters any more. I was tickled to see that one thing, at least, hadn't changed: when I asked where to discard a piece of wrapping paper, I got an exhaustive tour of his incredibly organized system for separating and storing recyclables.

Next morning after breakfast he asked, with transparent obliqueness, "What do you think I should do with all the tools and spare parts and junk down in the cellar?" My wife picked up on it and urged me to show an interest in his stuff. (You can have totally private conversations in the company of deaf people, as long as none of them read lips.)

"What's down there?" I asked, though I already knew. Come see, he replied, and we headed down the cellar stairs.

When he was a boy, deaf children in school were taught trades that didn't require much oral commu-nication. Printing was a favorite for boys. He learned it—composing, setting type, reading proof—and for the rest of his life has had at least one printing press in the cellar, where he's churned out stationery, busi-ness cards, and his monthly church bulletin. Now the equipment sits idle, probably at least a ton of it.

"Do you have any interest in any of this stuff?" he asked. He knew the answer, of course, or he wouldn't have asked. That stuff's been part of his life and his household for eighty years; he will leave the house forever before it does. Would it hurt him if I said no? I said no, and meant it.

We moved on to the work bench, a massive, antique oak Gibraltar with large, sticking drawers, and black as coal with age. It had been old in his boy-hood, still older in mine; and I can recall pinching the end of a finger in the handle of its vise when I was about five years old. Every square inch of horizontal space on its top and on the shelves above was covered with tools and spare parts—dozens of neatly labeled, dusty boxes of low-voltage switches, tin snips, transformers, electric vacuum cleaner motors, springs of all sizes, rusty brace bits, and my great-grandfather's cobbler's tools. Extension cords, like Christmas tree lights, plugged into adapters on the single electrical outlet off to one side.

Before the popularity of inexpensive electronic equipment, he'd been an electrical tinkerer. Beginning in his boyhood with six-volt dry cells and doorbell wire, he progressed to house current. When my sister and I were only infants, he learned from the neighbors—he and my mother, of course, couldn't hear us—that we were getting up at night to play. So he installed a switch that, when I opened my bedroom door, turned on a light in his bedroom. It occurs to me only now, as I think of it all these years later, that he could have told me I was under surveillance; but he preferred to catch me out. So it was as much a prank as a practical matter. But let that go now.

Later, when he had graduated to transformers, he manufactured "deaf doorbells" in his shop. Attached to the regular doorbell wiring and to several lights around the house, as well, they lit up houses like Times Square when someone came to the door. Unsuspecting brush salesmen were often startled by the display, and wondered what they'd done wrong.

Technology, however, caught up with him at last, as it does with all of us, and passed him by. Now all

those parts lay there on and around the bench—
relays, transformers, mercury switches, receptacles.
Virtually nothing of any usefulness, and yet virtually
nothing worthless. It was obvious that almost everything there had lost its utility for him, and just as
obvious that it would kill him to get rid of it. With
an empty cellar beneath him, stripped of his life's
collection of nuts, bolts, and doorbell wire, he would
be stranded, beached upstairs, useless and unable to
respond to household emergencies, one more stimu-
lus subtracted from his consciousness, waiting. We
sifted through everything without making plans for
anything. Only remembering.

Stay well, old man. In an hour, I'll be back home,
just upstairs from my own collection. I keep promis-
ing myself I'll go through it. But it costs so much to
get rid of things these days . . .

# You Can't Be a Grandfather

QUARTER PAST FIVE IN THE MORNING. The dog and I go through our daily ritual. She crouches in the hall until I finish in the bathroom, and shakes her tags impatiently when I say, "Whoops! Wait a minute! Water for the cat." The screen door opens; the cat comes in, and the dog and I go out. Down the driveway to the first place her nose arrests her. We check the night's haul of tracks. Two deer and a fox.

Back up the driveway with the paper, currently in twilight. The dog goes back to bed. I check the headlines, start the coffee, and put up my lunch. And about fifteen minutes later, I sit down happily to the news, fresh coffee, and a sausage-and-cheese omelet.

It's perfect—the quietest and most relaxing part of the day. Not a creature is stirring, and the phone probably won't ring until at least 6:30.

This morning, however, just about 5:45, I heard the whisper of bare feet on the stairs behind me— bare feet trying to sneak up on me, just as their mother's feet used to when she was little—and the mood was shattered. "Hi, Will," said my grandson. (I don't know whether that's a West Coast thing or a generational thing.) I was transformed in an eyeblink from a sage old gentleman enjoying his morning

94

paper into a hermit crab that's just been asked to share its shell. Emphasis on the crab.

Did you ever have to search for a rubber band, and finally find one, only to discover it'd lost its stretch? That with the slightest pressure it snapped, and kept on doing it, no matter how many knots you tied in it? Well, that's me as a grandfather.

I was too busy as a young man to do several of the things I enjoyed and was fairly good at. So I decided to save them for later years. I saved tennis, for example, for my fifties. Not a very bright idea. During that decade my knees disintegrated into crab meat; and the makers of tennis balls put a little extra jump on them. They moved much faster than they had when I was a kid.

I saved golf for my sixties. Also very dumb. Even though I'm exactly halfway in age between Arnie and Jack, when I swing a golf club, people around me start away in surprise. "What's that noise?" someone'll say. "Someone got a bag of potato chips?"

Similarly, I saved being a grandfather for later years. Like tennis and golf, it was bound to be something easy to do. Matter of fact, the word, "do," was irrelevant; grandfather was just something I'd be. Our kids would have kids, and those children would naturally yearn to spend time with the kindly, bearded old guy who knew so much, was so unbelievably wise, and loved to tell stories to the attentive little listeners clustered around his knees. It's a wonder that, during the time I was that naive, nobody sold me the Brooklyn Bridge.

This morning we were sitting on the deck in the sunshine. My wife (who missed a calling as a cruise ship activities director) handed me one of my favorite quasi-children's books, Barry Lopez's *Crow and Weasel.* She plopped the two grandsons down in front of me on the deck. "The boys," she assured all three of us, "would love to have you read this to them."

I must admit that they were gazing at me and the book with at least a modicum of interest. But *Crow and Weasel* is long for kids! I'd be amazed, I thought, if they got much past page 20.

I was wrong. About the end of page 3, the older one got up and walked firmly into the house. The screen door slapped behind him. I sneaked a glance at the five-year-old, who'd been pretty quiet. He was watching with rapt attention—like a hungry cougar watching a flock of sheep—the little green frogs down in Mother's garden pond.

"Okay," I said, "we'll pick this up later and finish it." He edged off toward the frogs. And later I found that we didn't need to pick it up; the older one already had, and finished it himself. I felt like a musical that had died in Connecticut.

Here's what happens if you and your grandchildren live far apart and see each other only now and then: You develop lives of your own. Not only are you two generations apart; you may be a nation apart, as well. You speak with different accents and operate in different contexts. If you're the older half of that equation, you've developed habits and boundaries that are difficult to break and painful to cross. Like the shoulders and knees that stiffen with lack of use, so do the lines of communication between you. In many ways you're the father you were, but more so.

Still, there are occasional little bursts of light.

Hiking the Appalachian Trail near our house one morning, one of them said, "I'd like to come here to see this in the winter." So I'm already making a note to get some snowshoe harnesses that'll fit his little boots. And last night Mother set us up again: The boys, she asserted, wanted to go fishing at the pond. We were taking a picnic.

Fishing! Holy Toledo! There was no way trout would hit in August. It'd be another disappointment, one more grandfatherly fantasy that wouldn't work out. Plus the thought of a $300 fly rod in the hands of a hyperactive five-year-old in a boat in the middle of a pond gave me major palpitations.

We drove to the pond. Mother set up the picnic on a table by the shore while I got out the biggest, most stable boat I could find. In respect of the boys' constant, squirming competitiveness—and I'd dared bring only one fishing rod—we decided to take out only one of them at a time. So one stayed ashore with Gramma, and five-year-old Riley went in the boat with me, holding the trolled line while his mother held the rod. It was a warm August evening, when trout traditionally lie doggo in the secret spring holes at the bottom of ponds. I rowed, desultorily and without much hope. Riley stared alternately at the trailing line between his fingers and at me, as if to ask why nothing had happened yet. His mother held the rod in one hand while her other hovered near the armpit of his life jacket, ready for anything.

Suddenly the line came to life. A great thrashing at the back of the boat as Riley and his mother, holding the rod and taking in line in clumsy fistfuls, hauled the trout toward the boat.

"Bring him around the side! Bring him around this side, and I'll net him," I cried. They did. I scooped him up in the soft catch-and-release net, removed the fly from his lip, and held him briefly up for admiration. "Hey! Nice rainbow! Good job, Riley!" I lowered the net into the water and let the fish swim out.

"Grampa Will!" I looked up into two huge, amazed eyes. "What'd you do?"

"Why, I let him go. I always do. Why?"

"That was my fish! I wanted to eat that fish!" Uh-oh.

"Oh, dear, I'm sorry," I said. "I didn't know that. Well, if you want one to eat, let's catch another one." I knew we wouldn't.

But we did. He was nervous as a cat until it was safely in the boat and quickly killed. I thought he'd be interested to see how I cleaned it, but he was standing up, dancing in place, and shouting announcements to his brother and grandmother over on the shore. "Thank you!" I murmured to the fish as I laid it under the seat.

He ate the fish the next evening. "You see this fish?" he asked everyone at the table. "This is my fish. I caught this fish. But this isn't the first fish I ever caught. Grampa Will threw away the first fish I ever caught. This is the second fish I ever caught."

They're coming again next summer. He wants to go fishing again. "But Grampa Will," he says, "this time I get to hold the rod myself, all right?"

This grandfather business is a piece of cake—as long as the fish cooperate.

# Gotcha Last!

WE BURIED OLD JAY LEWIS THE OTHER day, and now I'll never get even with him.

I don't mean that we just stuck him in a mausoleum till the spring thaw. I mean we buried him, right in ground frozen hard as steel. It was perfectly fitting, and appropriate to the life he'd lived, that when the subject of his funeral and interment came up at the meeting with Reverend Michaels, somebody volunteered to dig the hole. It happened to be Pete Bigelow, but it could have been any of us. "I'll dig the son of a gun," vowed Pete, with a mildness of expression unusual for him (in deference, no doubt, to the presence of the pastor). "I'll dig the son of a gun if I have to break every last tooth out of that brand-new backhoe bucket!"

For 45 years I was acquainted with the deceased, and he played with me pretty much the same game he played with everybody—sort of a one-up, gotcha game, you know. I used to think it was like chess, but it wasn't that complicated; it was one-on-one, no pawns involved. Checkers maybe, but it wasn't that friendly. It was most of all like that game of two-man tag that kids play, called "Got You Last." And the son of a bitch got me last.

He was a skinny, dyspeptic, green-and-brown

man: his skin, where it showed at his face and hands, was brown and liver-spotted; his shirt and pants always dark-green twill, with a matching greasy, green twill baseball cap askew on his head. His mouth was twisted into a perpetual sneer or snarl. You could see two brown teeth through it, a lateral and a bicuspid. Part of it was just the way he was; the other part was his stomach hurting him. Apparently it pained him something fierce most of the time. He took pills for it, but finally they had to take out part of his gut.

I never heard him laugh out loud but once in 45 years. That was down in front of the post office one day, when a Greyhound bus came roaring through the village and hit Hubert Roy's old bull bitch and left her screaming in the road.

So it was quite a surprise to see how many of us turned out for his services and even went to the graveside, cold as it was. 'Twas almost all men, and almost all of us dressed in wool frocks and pants, with old hunting licenses pinned to red-and-black-checked hats. There wasn't the usual chitchat you hear among old friends. I suppose each of us was going over his own private memories of his relationship with Jay Lewis.

Strange man. Nobody ever knew exactly where he'd come from. Somebody knew once, because he was actually a foundling, left in a soap box one winter day during the twenties on a doorstep over in Lewis. Hence the surname. His first name was the same as that of a town on the other side of the mountain. But that wasn't the last of his bad luck. The family that took him in lost everything in the Depression and moved away one night, and left that little kid behind, all by himself. I guess you could say he had a pretty tough start.

But as old Bill Broe used to say, "That only explains the way he is! It don't excuse it, god-dammit!" I don't know about that. But he was easily the ugliest-acting man I've ever known.

He hired out for room and board all through his boyhood, and then got a job as a superintendent and game protector for a private club with thousands of acres of forest land. And here he found his niche. No Doberman pinscher chained in a Jersey junkyard ever even approached the natural, enthusiastic, unremitting ferocity that Jay Lewis displayed in his chosen field.

Deer and trout, you know, are not cognizant of political boundaries. Nor are sportsmen, oftentimes. It occasionally befell that a local hunter, in the ardor of the chase, would cross the Club's frontier in his quest. And often as not, within a very few minutes he would look up into the triumphant sneer of the warden. Other times, he would return to his car to find all the valve stems removed from his tires. Gotcha last!

Naturally, we younger bloods took up the game with zest. We flooded his borders in mass incursions. After the snow was on the ground, we left tracks across Club land where we knew he'd find them, and jogged over a mountain or two on the way back to State land. Once we left a couple of brook trout on his back porch. He never caught any of us on these provocative expeditions—if he had, it would have meant a $25 fine for trespassing, and confiscation of our gear—but he always seemed to know who had left the tracks.

When he next met you at the post office, he'd say something like, "How's the huntin'? Pretty good?" Then, "Prob'ly be a lot better if you kept track of where you were headed." And he'd drill you with those eyes. Gotcha last!

He heard once that Ralph Ducharm had some venison in his woodshed. It wasn't even off Club land, either, and Ralph hadn't shot it. It was a gift, albeit illegal. The next day the troopers came and found it and took poor, harmless old Ralph over to the courthouse. None of us were friends of Ralph's. He was from our parents' generation, and a muscatel addict, besides. But that was lowdown meanness just for fun. So we vowed revenge.

His only weak spot besides his bad stomach, you see, was his intense zeal; in this he was predictable as the tide. And I had recently come into possession of about six feet of canvas belting from the sawmill down at the Forks.

We cut the belting into four pieces and drove about thirty long roofing nails through each piece. On a dark night in October we crept into his yard and laid a piece of belting, nail points up, on the ground right behind each wheel of his pickup. Then we hiked up onto the ridge across the valley and fired off two rifle shots that echoed through the valley like thunder.

"Bang!" went his screen door. We could imagine it all as if we were right there in his yard watching. His feet pounded down the porch steps. "Bang!" went the truck door. The motor raced. He wrenched the truck into reverse, popped the clutch, and backed fast out of his driveway. He shifted into first; and then there was the most satisfying "flop-flop-flop" sound that any of us had ever heard. If he had gotten out of his truck and run up the ridge after us, he would have caught us. We lay on the ground convulsed, absolutely unable to move.

He never mentioned the incident to anyone, which was ominous, but just like him. Then years later, he hired me one day to help him roof his woodshed. When I had my apron on, ready to climb up onto the roof, he handed me those four belts. "Here," he said, "use these nails. You prob'ly know how to get 'em out of there." Got you last.

Which meant it was my turn again. But with marriage and fatherhood, I wasn't quite as free as I had been, and my own fires were banked somewhat. So, though he remained ugly as ever to his dying day— he was the only man who ever asked to see my fishing license, as recently as last summer—I've been biding my time, waiting for the perfect opportunity. But, like everyone else gathered around that frozen hole in the ground last week, I won't get it now. He got us last.

Willem Lange was born in 1935. He has most of his hair and neither of his original knees.

Will first came to New England to prep school in 1950 as an alternative to reform school in his native New York State. During most of the time since, he has been collecting stories about the unique people and places in this surprisingly funny part of the world.

During a few absences from New England in the late fifties, Will managed to earn an undergraduate degree in only nine years at the College of Wooster in Ohio. In between those widely scattered semesters, he worked variously as a ranch hand, Adirondack guide, preacher, construction laborer, bobsled run announcer, assembly line worker, cab driver, bookkeeper, and bartender. After finally graduating in 1962, he taught high school English for six years, filling in summers as an Outward Bound instructor.

From 1968 to 1972 Will directed the Dartmouth Outward Bound Center. Since 1972 he has been a building and remodeling contractor in Hanover, New Hampshire.

In 1981 he began writing a weekly column, "A Yankee Notebook," which appears in several New England newspapers. Since 1993 he has been a regular commentator on Vermont Public Radio. And his annual readings of Charles Dickens' *A Christmas Carol* are now in their twenty-fifth year.

In 1973 Will founded the Geriatric Adventure Society, a loosely knit group of outdoor enthusiasts whose members have skied in the two-hundred-mile Alaska Marathon, climbed in the Andes and Himalayas, bushwhacked on skis through most of northern New Hampshire, and paddled rivers north of the Arctic Circle in Canada.

He and his wife, Ida, who is the proprietor of a kitchen design business, were married in 1959. They live on a dead-end dirt road in Etna, New Hampshire, and have three children and four grandchildren.

LIBRARY OF CONGRESS CATALOGING-IN-PUBLICATION DATA

Lange, Willem, 1935–
    Okay, let's try it again  / by Willem Lange.
        p.   cm.
    "The pieces in this book first appeared in the Valley News,
    Lebanon, New Hampshire"—T.p. verso.
    ISBN 1–58465–004–4 (pbk.   :   alk. paper)
    1. Lange, Willem, 1935–   —Friends and associates.
2. Lange, Willem, 1935–   —Anecdotes.
3. United States—Social life and customs Anecdotes.   I. Title.
CT275.L2723A3   1999
973.9'092—dc21                                             99–34966